Questions from the City, Answers from the Forest

Questions from the City, Answers from the Forest

Simple Lessons You Can Use from a Western Buddhist Monk

Ajahn Sumano Bhikkhu

A publication supported by
THE KERN FOUNDATION

Quest Books
Theosophical Publishing House

Wheaton, Illinois ◆ Chennai (Madras), India

The Theosophical Publishing House
P. O. Box 270
Wheaton, IL 60189-0270

A publication of the Theosophical Publishing House,
a department of the Theosophical Society in America

Library of Congress Cataloging-in-Publication Data

Ajahn Sumano, Bhikkhu.
 Questions from the city, answers from the forest: simple lessons you
can use from a Western Buddhist monk / Ajahn Sumano Bhikkhu.
  p.   cm.
ISBN 0-8356-0774-7
1. Religious life—Buddhism.
BQ5395.A33   1999
294.3'444—dc21   99-11828
                                                          CIP

4   3   2   1   *   99   00   01   02   03   04   05

Printed in the United States of America

CONTENTS

Introduction

The questions and answers in this book have been taken from dozens of journals and diaries compiled during my twenty years of monastic practice. The questions originated from the hearts of other spiritual seekers whom I have happened to meet along the way. The questions were directed to me, and I responded to them as best as I could, treating each with respect, and knowing that if my mind is empty, I will be free to respond to the essence of the question and the need of the questioner in that moment.

Looking back, I recognize the truth that sincere inquiry always sparks our movement toward truth and compassion. Deep questions that arise naturally in the process of life's unfolding signal the manifestation of the very energy through which we grow further. We would be arrogant to believe that we can proceed far without pondering the important questions life asks of us.

How did my karma bring me the opportunity to answer such questions? And how did I come to this place? And why did I come?

I was born in Chicago in 1940. My family had Jewish roots, though a mixed ethnic heritage. Our neighbors were mostly Catholic—Italians, Poles, and Irish. It was an interesting experience to grow up in a predominantly Catholic neighborhood at that time. An undercurrent of anti-Semitism was always lurking about, which generated confusion in the minds of my friends and myself. The heart of the problem was that since we were not aware that there was any difference between being a Jew and not a Jew, we couldn't understand what was wrong with being one.

Two significant experiences came out of that somewhat confused identity. When I was a little boy, my grandfather, who spoke only Russian and Yiddish, took me regularly to a tiny, unheated Orthodox synagogue. There I would be squashed between two gigantic, bearded old men garbed in heavy, full-length black woolen coats, with skullcaps on their heads and prayer shawls over their shoulders. The mingled smells of perspiration and wool and adult bodies moving in prayer were at once awful and wonderful. Being wedged in there between these old men, who were alternately sitting and nodding, half-bowing and standing, touched me profoundly and connected me to something safe and beautiful. After passing through all the business of my youth and adolescence, I would search all over the world for similar mystical experiences.

The second important experience that has remained with me was the intuitive understanding that to be a Jew was to be a person who seeks God. Being a member of the "chosen people" meant that one had the authority and permission to do that. I also knew, even if it was heretical to think this, that everyone was a Jew in this regard and that searching for God was a sign that one was chosen. For me, being a Jew was about not a religion but a calling; being chosen meant that God was the priority in one's life. Later, I knew enough to express this insight in Buddhist language: to be chosen meant that one had arrived, through unfathomable lifetimes spent in the service of goodness, at a lifetime in which one would have the opportunity to seek and the sensitivity to develop that positive potential.

I completed grade school and high school in an ordinary way. From the age of ten until my teen years, I was encouraged and groomed to become an amateur boxer by our neighbors, who were boxing promoters and managers. While they watched prominent fighters work out in the gym, they would assign some jaded (and usually loopy, punch-drunk) guy to give me lessons. I fought in some Golden Gloves events, managing to win a few. The other sport in which I invested time was bowling. I believe my classmates and their bowling fathers still remember me as the kid who bowled the highest game in the junior league: 277. For ten years, that record stood as the highest score for bowlers under eighteen across the country.

A third significant experience occurred in my teen years. One day, when I was fourteen, I noticed a carousel of paperback books in a drug store. I had never seen books displayed like that before. At that age I didn't go to bookstores—though I frequented school libraries and read more than anyone I knew—so this was the first rack of books I had encountered. My eyes went right to three books on Buddhism: one by Alan Watts, another by Christmas Humphreys, and a third by D. T. Suzuki. They were inexpensive paperbacks, so I bought them all. I read these books six or seven times each within a month, missing a week of school in the process. I was enthralled. They confirmed what I intuited to be the nature of the world. But in the turbulent years that followed, when hormones began turning my attention to school proms, clothes, cars, and the like, this spark of spiritual interest was subdued. It wouldn't be reignited for fifteen years.

In college, first at the University of Illinois and later at the University of Miami and DePaul University, I followed the directions of my family and high school advisors and spent years studying only things that I wasn't interested in, including three years of law school. Back in Chicago after a year of service in the Naval Reserve, I began working in real estate. I fully expected that if I applied myself to the pursuit of success and money, hard work and dedication would pay off handsomely. I married, my new wife and I settled into a comfortable life, and we lived happily ever after—that is, for about four years. We had no children—*we* were the children.

By twenty-nine, I recognized that business ability coupled with a driving ambition had effectively trapped me. Either I had to turn away from this never-ending, never-resting lifestyle, forfeiting the large commissions still owed me, or stay with it until I dropped dead behind an antique oak desk, stacks of files, and three telephones.

Walking through Chicago's Loop one miserable winter morning, I noticed a collage of photos in the window of the Pan Am Airlines office. The photos, seemingly taken of every sunny beach in the world, surrounded an ad for a round-the-world ticket—$1249, good for one year. I stopped and stared, edging closer to see more detail of the beach photos. Two days later, on an equally windy, sloshy day, I passed by the Pan Am office again, on the way to an important appointment. After a frustrating and energy-draining morning, I closed up my briefcase and came out for air.

I purposely returned by way of Pan Am. This time I went in, picked up a brochure, and leafed through it for some minutes. I approached the counter and said to the smiling agent, "I'll take two, please"—one for myself and the other for my wife. After that, everything happened very quickly. Once I recognized that the guiding principle had to be not wanting the whole catastrophe of my job to be waiting for me when I returned, I left everything at work to my employees and business associates.

Leaving from O'Hare International Airport, surrounded by friends and acquaintances who couldn't believe this was really happening, was comical. Everyone assured us we'd be back inside of two months, bored by travel and homesick for Chicago. We boarded the plane, I took off my necktie for the last time, and we were on our way.

Almost two years later, we returned and settled in Arcata, California, joining a friend there who was teaching at a university. But those two years, spent mostly in India and other parts of Asia, had irrevocably transformed my outlook toward just about everything. Coming home, I could not find a place where I could fit in. Nor could our marriage assimilate all that had happened— and my wife and I went our separate ways.

I began practicing yoga, took up running, explored psychotherapy, studied phenomenology, spent weeks motorcycle-camping in Oregon and Washington, and experimented with psychedelics. The images of Buddhas and figures of monks that I had found so compelling in my travels dominated my mind. Eventually, I became affiliated with several yoga ashrams and moved into one that was a branch of the American Sikh movement.

After eight months with the Sikhs, complete with an eight-month beard, a turban, and a little hooked knife, another yogi and I moved to San Francisco to join the Sufi community there. In that year, I learned Sufi dancing, several forms of massage therapy, and some acupuncture and homeopathy. By now, I had become a vegetarian, quit smoking and drinking wine, and had taken a vow of celibacy. The Sufi community was spread up and down the Northern California coast, from San Jose to Ukiah. I decided to settle in Palo Alto to make use of Stanford University's libraries. But now, instead of just browsing through Buddhist books, I was taking notes. When I came upon the books of Alan Watts, Christmas Humphreys, and D. T. Suzuki, everything re-kindled, most especially my earlier fascination with the Buddhist path.

Soon I was off to Taos, New Mexico, to attend the first re-treat led by the founding teachers of the Insight Meditation Soci-ety (IMS), who included Jack Kornfield, Joseph Goldstein, and Sharon Salzburg. Notwithstanding one day spent in continuous crying, I managed to survive the ten days. I was encouraged to fly to Massachusetts to take part in IMS's first three-month retreat in its new center. Those three months led to almost three years of retreats under various IMS teachers, with occasional seven- to ten-day Zen retreats at different centers led by visiting Japanese and Korean teachers.

Meditation practice made my mind clear, soft, and rela-tively content. But I also felt the need to grow. So I decided to go back to India, with a stop in Great Britain. India held out the hope of finding some obscure teacher somewhere in the Himalayas who could point to the way out of the cycle of suffering

Buddhists call *samsara*. I was determined to endure any hardship and go to any length in order to meet such a master. I had yet to come upon one in whom I had that kind of confidence.

I left Boston bound for India, expecting to have to virtually crawl over the Himalayas naked to find my teacher. Instead, I met a meditation teacher from IMS living in London who invited me to meet five Western monks—Americans and Canadians—who were disciples of the well-known Thai meditation master, Ajahn Cha. At first I resisted the invitation. Visiting monks in their beat-up British monastery was not on my itinerary. However, my friend, who hung around this monastery every day, kept urging me to accompany him, so I eventually gave in. My first visit led to daily visits, then to a postponement of my trip to India, until I put the idea of continuing on to India completely away for awhile. Finally, I moved in to help out as a cook, and soon after began training there.

Three years later I was the first monk to be ordained in the newly constructed monastery, which had taken seven years to complete. In my fifth "rains," as Theravada Buddhists (the southern school of Buddhists) term the annual three-month retreat, I left for Thailand a fully ordained *bhikkhu*.

I still live in northeast Thailand alone in a cave, devoting a good part of my days and nights to sitting and walking meditation, following the tradition of the forest mendicants—a practice identical to that which the Buddha himself formulated after his enlightenment.

At present there are about fifteen hundred monks living in this tradition, spread out in three to four hundred meditation monasteries. Outside of Thailand, branches of this tradition exist in the United States, Great Britain, Switzerland, Australia, New

Zealand, and Sri Lanka. Ordained monks come from every Western country—there is even one Native American—and others come from Russia, Czechoslovakia, and Israel. There is keen and growing interest in ordination among women as well. And, as with the men, those women who take ordination are staying in robes for longer and longer periods of time.

While meditation monks and nuns prefer to stay in the forest, they also recognize the need for Dharma in modern society. In that spirit, in the past few years I have been traveling and teaching for two to three months each year. And during the monsoon season, I join with a small group of forest monks for the annual three-month rains retreat, which begins on the full moon of July.

In 1994–1995, the opportunity to teach Dharma found its way to my forest cave. English-speaking tourists at a guest house in nearby Kowyai National Park were eager to meet a Western Buddhist monk. When the guest house hosts asked me to give a little talk and to answer some questions, I agreed. I conducted talks there on probably twenty occasions, mostly to Westerners who had little or no familiarity with Buddhist teachings.

The questions asked by these "city" people were always interesting, both for the questions themselves and for what they revealed about the questioners. Sometimes people ask questions to display their intellectual prowess, often missing a genuine opportunity to expand their minds and, instead, falling deeper into the abyss of self. Questions asked merely to accumulate knowledge just add more burden to our already encumbered lives—more data, more trivia, more bytes to sift through in order to get to the present. These questions failed to catch my attention or arouse energy and empathy, and so have gone unrecorded.

Other questions have a ring of humility. They silence the self. These questions open the mind, turn it around, soften it, and make it pliable. They are profound in their asking and remain profound eternally. These are the questions that have been given shelter and space in this book. I have recorded them with the aim of providing an easily accessible reference tool for maintaining spiritual consciousness in the midst of a busy world. Combining these questions with contemplation can push the mind beyond thought, for with thought alone it is not possible to arrive at the truth we seek.

Some of the selections in this book have been gleaned from my personal notes. I've kept these questions and their answers at hand because I have found value in referring to them over the years. They came back to me in moments of need and confusion, when I had forgotten what I knew in other moments. So, ironically, some of these answers became benchmarks in my own practice.

Reviewing my notes with other people, many of them said that the questions and answers reflected their own path of inquiry. I decided that it would be useful to make this material more widely available so that others might have an opportunity to study these questions and answers. Soon after that decision was made, several people offered to transcribe these conversations. It is through the energy of these "bodhisattvas" that the original notes were finally assembled into manuscript form.

Later, an old battery-operated Mac laptop computer made its way into my life in my cave. For the most part, I worked on the book in forty-minute increments. This was all the power the computer's battery had before it needed recharging. So, there was a day for writing, followed by a day for recharging, followed by another day for writing. These limitations served to keep my mind focused and kept the project from distracting me from the sixteen-hour daily meditation schedule I have maintained for years.

As the collated materials started to take shape, I realized that the sequence of questions and answers provided readers with an introduction to Buddhist ideas and a way of applying these ideas to various categories of human concern. I hope that this little book can shed some light on these, in the midst of the confusion and frustration inherent in cultures that suppress and deny our Buddha-nature. Perhaps the comments and considerations contained in some of these conversations will awaken you to "the-way-things-are," the truth inside you that is just waiting for your reflection and appreciation. Many of my students have used focused inquiry as a means to move beyond a stagnant situation. This kind of self-exploration nudges us along such that we blossom into sensitive and loving beings. Once we recognize the value of truth, the gate to wisdom is thrown open and enlightenment becomes a real possibility.

Solitude, simplicity, and intense introspection—these are some of the aspects of Buddhist meditation that I have emphasized over the years. But while living in a cave as a monk can provide the ideal environment for these kinds of practices, being a lay person should not be considered a drawback to enlightenment. To live in caring and sensitive relationship with others develops the faculties that allow enlightenment to happen. No one can make enlightenment happen. We just have to live wisely; incline our lives toward truth; continuously undercut and diminish selfishness; and develop poise, alertness, and kindness so that the real, loving, compassionate being who we are can be here in this present moment, where enlightenment can happen.

PART ONE

Questions from the City

What now, Brothers, is the Noble Truth of Suffering?

Birth is suffering; decay is suffering; death is suffering; sorrow, lamentation, pain, grief, and despair are suffering; not to get what one desires is suffering; in short, the Five Aggregates of Existence are suffering.

THE WORD OF THE BUDDHA
—*Ven. Nyanatiloka Thera*

The truth of suffering is a universal experience, for it is some-thing inherent in the very fabric of life itself. What we make of this realization, however, is what will ultimately determine our spiritual fate: yet another round of rebirth in a million more rounds—or, finally, the exit to that realm of highest bliss, permanently and eternally beyond the reach of suffering.

CHAPTER ONE

Turning to Spiritual Life

Q: As you see it, what is the best way to walk through this world?

A: Your way. You must pursue your life according to the stream of your karma, which will pretty much dictate the manner and mode of your life. It will incline you toward particular vocations and obscure openings into others. That's your karmic destiny. But if all you do is go along with it, you won't have much spiritual leverage on your life. You will be pushed from behind by a litany of "likes," which you will go after, and "dislikes," which you will turn away from.

When you have matured enough to reflect upon your life experience—and at this point meditation is very helpful—you will be able to gain a greater perspective and see a larger horizon at the frontier of human potentiality. You will begin to see that there is a grander life outside the limitations of one's karmic inheritance, and you will want to explore this dimension.

This is the awakening state. You carry on living your life as you have been doing. From the outside, everything appears to be the same. However, your focus has now shifted from the events of the outside world to the mechanisms and movements that trigger your thoughts and actions. You turn your attention to cause rather than effect. This is the awareness of a person who knows that he or she has been wounded by a poison arrow and is no longer struggling to suppress the suffering from that poison but rather seeks a cure to the toxicity of the poison itself. Those who overcome the effects of the poison or avoid it altogether are the sages and noble ones who have walked this world in the wisest of ways.

Q: Is there a particular set of factors that, when they come together, constitute a kind of spiritual flash point? Or said differently, are there certain experiences, such as the death of a friend or family member, that turn the mind out of its normal, foolish way of behaving?

A: There is no particular set of circumstances. But adversity, separation from loved ones, aging, and the death of intimate companions have more spiritual impact on the mind than does the relatively pain-free yet semi-conscious state of mind we have when everything is just skimming along. When life is easy, we tend to be absorbed in the things of the moment, just letting the good times roll. But every good roll ends. If this weren't the case, the saga of human beings on this planet would be entirely different.

The factors that stimulate awakening depend upon a person's karma. They also depend to a large extent upon the times. Several generations ago a key factor would have been the world wars. A generation ago there was widespread disappointment in many Western countries as the era of far-left liberal political ideologies drew to an end. I experienced that myself. A wave of hope and enthusiasm had crashed and burned, causing a fallout of considerable disillusionment and suffering, and leaving many intelligent and sensitive people adrift. When people see their hopes and visions collapse, they often turn inward to religion and spirituality.

At present, an awakening to the critical need for spirituality often arises just because of the chaos of daily living. Life at the end of the twentieth century is particularly full of stress and anxiety. The quality of our environment has drastically degenerated. When people can no longer see the moon and the stars or enjoy the trees and flowers, life becomes acutely distressful, and even psychotic. The unsuitable living conditions of most cities have driven people to seek a more sane way of life, mostly through meditation and spiritual practice. People are very much aware that there is something basically wrong at the core of contemporary society.

In my own case, I had become conscious of the ever-changing mix of success and failure in my life. I didn't like failure, so I struggled for continual success—an impossible goal, of course. What I found even more distressing was the fact that within success itself there was failure. There was winning, yet I wasn't winning. This led me to look at things more deeply. And this inevitably led to spiritual reflection and the yearning to embrace a spiritual lifestyle.

So, one doesn't have to look for a special set of factors for awakening to arise. Right smack in the middle of daily life, if one looks into it carefully, lie the seeds of discontentment. The suffering inherent in all aspects of an unenlightened life signals the need to find a radical approach to living, one that transcends and transforms the heart.

Q: I am a businessman with a computer software company, and so far we are a success. I have learned a great deal about electronics, administration, public relations, and all the other skills involved in running this kind of business. But someday I hope to cash in my stock and begin another life. I will probably study the various Eastern religions, as they attract me. I want to find peace of mind.

A: Your life's story sounds similar to mine. If I were you, I wouldn't wait for "someday," for it may never come. You seem to be one of those people of the postmodern age who know all there is to know about the world but haven't the faintest idea of who they are. You know how to market a product, how to surf the Internet, the number of bonus points you get for renting a car from Avis, and the price of airline tickets all over the world. But you don't know what you are, how you came to be born, where you are going, the meaning and purpose of life, and how it came to be that even though you are successful, you live in turmoil and sorrow while your spirit longs for peace and happiness.

You are living your life backwards. You should first attend

to these questions. I hazard a guess that if you looked carefully at your situation, you would find that you have already accumulated enough of what you think you need to be able to quit. Go-getters like yourself can withdraw from the business world knowing that you have the fortitude and skills to come back again and build up another business. Decide to stop in six months and you'll see that in six months, conditions will have arranged themselves so you can let go. Once you are out from under all that, you will move into a better, grander life. You will be ready to examine your life. Realize the truth of your life and you will find what you really want—peace.

A man came to visit me more out of curiosity about the way I live than interest in why I live as I do. He didn't know much about Buddhism. He had read that Buddhism says life is an immersion in suffering and conflict. This immediately turned him off from any further inquiry. Yet there remained some part of him that wouldn't turn away.

We talked casually about the weather, the changes in Thai culture over the past few years, and, of course, Bangkok's famous traffic jams. After a while, he got around to asking me if it was true that the Buddhist religion sees life as a sea of suffering. I guess he wanted to confirm his understanding but felt confined by the religious norms he was accustomed to. A fear hung over him that deviating from what he had been taught as a child would land him in hell. Thus it's not surprising that he was reluctant to step outside the boundaries of his faith and look into another.

I took his question as the inquiry of someone who would really like to know more about life. I asked him, "Is there suffering in your life? Do you experience suffering in your daily living?" He answered, "No, not really. Sometimes things go well, sometimes they don't. A lot of the time things just go along."

I responded, "I'm not asking you how things go. I am asking you about your emotional and psychological states in the course of the day. Are you aware of how much pain you go through in a day? Have you ever counted the sad moments that arise in just one twenty-four-hour period? How much of your day do you spend floundering in doubt, fear, or anxiety? When you find that you have made a mistake or can't decide where to have lunch, are you at ease?

"When you go home, close your eyes and observe the moments of pain that manifest in your mind, in your heart. Just count the flashes of disappointment, regret, anxiety, fear, and confusion that infiltrate your mind in one day. Only if you don't see a continuous pattern of such dis-eased thoughts can you truthfully say that there is no suffering in your world."

The teachings of the Buddha are nothing less than a foolproof approach to eradicating the whole mass of suffering. They provide a window of opportunity for escaping from the endless wheel of birth and death and birth again.

Q: My life is continually filled with problems. I never seem to be able to get out from under them.

A: I have heard you complain about your problems many times. And I keep telling you that you are fooled into believing that certain situations are problematic.

Look instead to bigger problems—for instance, the problem of life and death. If you contemplate this greater problem, your so-called problems will fade away. I'm not saying that they will stop appearing. They will go on for sure. But you will see them in a way that will help resolve the questions surrounding your very life and death.

Q: Why do I feel so unstable most of the time?

A: Because right from the start you are trying to grasp things. This is bound to make you feel restless and topsy-turvy. You are easily drawn toward things, which in the long run creates a no-win situation. If you don't get what you want, you are disappointed or even despondent. Then, after you have accepted the situation and collected and consolidated your energies, you're off on another happiness-seeking offensive. When you finally get what you want, you are happy. But it is momentary, the kind of happiness that makes you restless. Think about the lyrics to all those love songs we hear on the radio. Do you think that the love they are glorifying will bring enduring happiness? Do you think that if people actually could manifest their hopes and dreams, they really would go on to love someone else forever? No way. Winning happiness merely at the worldly level necessarily brings more agitation.

The insatiability of greed, the heat that comes from endless desire, the illusion of a real self, the incessant presence of change in this world—these need to be contemplated. Not in the head, but in the heart. If we don't know their nature, we don't stand a chance of finding happiness.

As an example, I know a woman who felt she needed to succeed and make her mark in the world. She did this. Then she needed a long retreat to recover. Then she needed a new lifestyle: a house in the country, a dog, a man, a baby, a four-wheel-drive Jeep. Then she needed another change and a retreat, and so the cycle began again. And ended. And then began again. Every three to four years I get a letter from her when she is at the end of one of these cycles. Now she is married again and living abroad. Not yet happy, of course. She is destined to continue to spin around until she comes to seek a change not in the external world but in her heart.

Q: I'm fed up with the world. It is depressing, disgusting, and obscene. I am ready and eager to begin my search for enlightenment. Now what? Where should I go? I need your advice.

A: Actually, you don't need to go anywhere. Going here and there will just spin you back into the very world that so pains you. But I can see that you cannot understand this yet. If I tell you that all that you need to discover is closer than the tip of your nose, you won't understand what I am alluding to.

Like those who have gone before you on the path to enlightenment, you need to begin at the beginning. Begin by living simply and morally. This cultivates the ground in which concentration can develop. You should try to spend time in natural surroundings, where the environment helps to settle the mind. As the mind cools and quiets down, insight will begin to develop. Insight is a characteristic of a mind able to concentrate. You will begin to see that you are on your way.

What I just said answers your question of how to go about your spiritual quest. As to where to go, I would suggest first attending a meditation retreat. In a ten-day or two-week retreat you will find some moments of silence and experience a few moments of peace, which are not part of your usual busy life.

After you have had time to digest the effects of the first retreat, take a second one. If the teachers of these courses are able to encourage and guide you in observing the nature of change and suffering and the fact of no self, you will be pointed in a new direction. If the teachers are mature practitioners, they will be excellent examples of the benefits that meditation brings to a human life. I believe that we human beings learn best by example. That is, we learn respect and admiration for the Buddha-Dharma, the teachings of the Buddha, from those who exhibit the light of awareness.

The world and the meditative environment face in opposite directions. The five senses, along with the mind, pick up stimuli, which produce feelings. If we search for satisfaction and happiness in these feelings, we are engaged in a hopeless and helpless endeavor. Pleasant music can stimulate feelings of pleasure. Lovely forms can bring pleasure to us based on the beauty and attractiveness of a form. Pleasing tastes work the same way. The mental pictures and video tapes that memory plays back for us can be pleasant experiences as well. That is why we dither around in our memory banks. But all of these are temporary. The pleasant things we search for are time-dated. They run out. Hooked on wanting more of the same, we will run to the refrigerator, call a friend, play another song, switch on the TV, or just lie on our bed and conjure up a beaten-to-death romantic moment out of our adolescence.

Sincere seekers begin to lose confidence in this way of living. They turn inward, away from the beckoning of a chaotic and confused world. If they take up the practice of meditation with the same kind of enthusiasm to excel that they bring to learning the piano or practicing ping-pong, they will succeed in the practice. Their meditation practice will develop steadily, and their perspective on the world will shift into harmony with the-way-things-are. What is really important in a human life, and what activities lead to happiness and peace and which ones lead down a futile road to nowhere, all become clear.

Chapter Two

The World through a Seeker's Eyes

Q: Just look around at all the marvels brought into the world by science and technology. Are you not impressed?

A: I'm not so much impressed as depressed. Look beyond the invention of all this marvelous and powerful technology. How is it being used?

I am using the word *depressed* more as an expression than to refer to an attitude of mind. My mind no longer becomes depressed over the tragic misuse of nature. Nothing can alter this course; it is the way it is.

Q: What is the cause of all the wars erupting at this time?

A: Who can say? These events have innumerable karmic tentacles that connect the past to the present and the present to the future. A supercomputer couldn't trace all the factors creating any one event. This planet is full of dangers. All kinds of deadly toys are set to go off, and many of these dangerous things are in the hands of crazy people—or angry people, which amounts to the same thing.

But the world isn't dangerous just because crazy men have arsenals of chemical and nuclear weapons, or because angry, vengeful demons control fleets of nuclear submarines and long-range missiles. The great and present danger is the fact that our minds are out of control. Each of us still trapped and living under the sway of our defilements is in a state of jeopardy. Anyone in this situation can fall into the lower realms of life energy and become a raging demon or a denizen of the hell realms. These realms are actually states of being that we can and do experience in our everyday life—fortunately not for long. If we practice properly, we can put a cap on these states of experience and abide continuously in peace.

Stop the war within yourself and you will do the world and humanity the greatest service.

Q: Why do political agreements, sweated and hammered out after hours and hours of negotiations, collapse? In the end, all the dialogue, all the wheeling and dealing, and all the promises come to nothing.

A: Because the people involved in these agreements have no political integrity. Perhaps *political integrity* is an oxymoron; politics and integrity are in two altogether different domains. We shouldn't expect much good to come out of the political arena, for the different parties don't agree to participate within an honest, moral, and ethical framework. There isn't much common ground. No side has the intention to give away anything of real value.

Personally, I don't follow the news, so I am not emotionally affected by world events.

The political playing field doesn't evoke honor or integrity, does it? Essentially, diplomatic meetings and conferences only aim to keep the leaders from being too selfish or barbaric. When you come to see that politics are inherently unstable and inconclusive, you won't be disappointed by the failure of accords, contracts, peace process covenants, and the like. Indeed, it is amazing when the parties involved can resolve even the smallest conflict. Your description of the bargaining process as "hammering away" speaks to the power politics that the representatives employ in their negotiations. When agreements are put together in the name of power, intimidation, and exploitation, they fall apart when the power shifts. On the other hand, agreements put together out of compassion, mutual respect, and selflessness thrive and endure.

If I were mediating a discussion between political opponents, I would have them sit together for twenty to thirty minutes before any talking began. This would raise the level at which the participants meet, and they would have an opportunity to meet more productively.

Q: What would you say are the significant factors in bringing about the paucity of political vision we Americans are currently experiencing?

A: Unless a government acts along time-honored guidelines that reflect natural wisdom, it will not be able to function on behalf of the people. Unless the leaders follow these guidelines, no clear vision of the future can emerge. What arises instead is a murky, distorted, limited view that only sees things in the short term.

The Buddha laid out seven basic principles that any government is ethically obligated to fulfill:

1. Meeting regularly and often to confer on pertinent matters.

2. Coming together, conducting meetings, and dispersing in harmony.

3. Adhering to the laws laid down in the constitution.

4. Honoring and respecting elders.

5. Honoring and respecting women, children, and the disabled, and protecting them from abuse.

6. Honoring and serving holy places and national shrines and traditions.

7. Organizing protection, sanctuary, and rightful support for the religious.

When there is collective concern for these matters, the people will be able to manifest a sensitive, intelligent vision that the government will be obliged to follow. I don't think a government can function properly as guardian of the happiness and security of its citizens unless it is operating with these principles as its standard.

We can speak of the world as multi-dimensional. That is, there are parallel perceptions of the world operating simultaneously. What you see is what you are tuned in to.

For instance, we can involve ourselves in political matters or spiritual matters. These two perspectives of the same world differ radically from each other. The majority of people today have chosen to see and be in the world politically. This implies participation in world events that trouble the mind and heart. Bosnia, Israel, Iraq, Ireland, Rwanda, Colombia, Korea—the problems plaguing these and other countries never seem to go away. Nightmare scenarios are recycled, with minor variations, coming back onto the world stage for another round in the spotlight. Obviously, the way these problems are approached is critically flawed.

The difficulty lies with the politicians and with the people who consider these problems with political consciousness. By contrast, when we approach a problem from a spiritual perspective, we come to that problem with a willingness to make intelligent and appropriate sacrifices in order to allow others to be happy and feel secure. We let go of the idea that they are the enemy, that they are *other* in relation to us. We recognize that their predicament is not unlike our own.

Politically, one side loses. Spiritually, everyone wins. Giving up and letting go stimulates a similar response from the world, one way or another. Then comes the inclination for real justice, true goodness and fairness, and genuine bonding between diverse people in mutual respect. A spiritual perspective carries with it an appreciation of the karmic struggle all living beings have to confront. Everyone will grow old, become ill, and die. Only a few human beings will live beyond ninety years of age.

When all parties recognize the poignancy of the vulnerability of life, they can live together in an environment less clogged with fear and distrust. We are truly brothers and sisters here. With this in mind, agreements, treaties, mandates, or whatever we call these contracts between people are maintained and preserved.

It would be naive to expect that the world should simply begin to function in this way. We can only take our own stance in this perspective and bring forth its principles before others. The most powerful thing we can do to soothe the world and move it forward is to radiate loving kindness. When there is enough loving kindness in the world, this gentle but powerful force will generate a shift in consciousness, prompting an understanding of the value of and the need for peace.

This is wonderful mental training. Even if we don't see the result in the outside world, we can feel it within ourselves. Life mellows and becomes more and more a simple opportunity for offering. When we approach people and situations with an interest in giving, we recognize that this is far more satisfying than receiving.

Recognizing the value of giving, we enter right into the heart of the Buddha's teaching. We honor ourselves by functioning with wisdom and compassion. We honor ourselves by giving up things for the benefit of others. This doesn't mean that we should sign away the house. It is simply an operative principle that we can apply to all our life situations. We develop our life according to our environment and our karmic situation. We use our talents and abilities to rise above base instincts and selfish conditioning. We become less interested in dominating and winning than in acceptance, contentment, and the simplicity of letting go.

Q: What's the point of spreading loving kindness in the world? The world is only getting darker and things are degenerating more and more. Wars are becoming a common occurrence. There is increasing conflict between neighboring countries, let alone between the powerful, nuclear countries, and millions suffer from hunger and displacement. What's the use of trying?

A: All this is true. On the other hand, what we read about and see on the evening news is just a sliver of reality. We can look at the news as another product fabricated and marketed to the consumer. Wars are presented as accepted events by the media. We aren't shown much about efforts toward peace, nor much about interest in it either.

The momentum of hatred and fear generates an environment of distrust. When somebody offends somebody else, the offender is assaulted. This triggers a cycle of revenge attacks, and so it goes—Serbs hating Croats, Indians and Pakistanis distrusting each other, Tutsis and Hutus bent on genocide, Sinhalese and Tamils unable to share an island. So many scores to settle. Where is the letting go? Where is the goodness that shames hatred?

We all have a duty to spread *metta,* loving kindness, in the world. We must practice *metta* in all situations, because the world is bigger than this planet and time is greater than the events of this era. When we walk about, we walk for peace. When we sit, we sit for peace. When we work or speak with others, it is with a heart inclined toward peace. We make our own world peaceful and harmless so that peace can spread out from right here and right now—from consciousness. This effort appears seemingly insignificant in a world where tens of thousands of bullets are expended, and hundreds of mines blow the limbs off children daily. But the spreading of loving kindness, if done with great purity, has a profound effect. Mother Teresa was a great example. Whatever else she may have done through her social service, her loving kindness was what the world marveled at.

The inner peace that we are all capable of radiating into the world is the energy that transforms people's hearts and minds. We sit to meditate with a heart full of *metta* because it has a great influence upon ourselves, our friends, and our society. It protects our personal world from dangers and builds peace-bridges to the larger world. The peace-bridges built today and tomorrow will gradually extend into the future. There will be a time when the horrors of this era will be forgotten. Our *metta* today will help pave the way, and may even be the critical factor in this transformation.

Q: As a social worker, I want to ask you just one question: what is normal?

A: The way things are.

You see it is easy to ask this question but impossible to really answer it. As a social worker, you would have already asked yourself, "What can be done for the world? What are the root problems of the world? How can I help?" Perhaps as yet you haven't found satisfactory answers. A penetrating mind won't find satisfaction in looking at these questions conventionally. These questions have to be seen from the bottom up, so to speak. You have to understand something about the nature of the world, the nature of the mind, the causes of problems and conflicts, and the way beyond problems and conflicts.

The understanding that transforms the way you see the world comes out of a radical restructuring of your view of reality. Then the ability to recognize what to do in any situation becomes normal.

Though tens of thousands of people have been working for at least a thousand years to try to improve society, it continues in its overall miserable state of injustice, exploitation, and intimidation. While some segments of society have progressed slightly, any improvement of the general quality of human life has only been cosmetic.

If there is to be a significant improvement in the quality of our personal and societal life, it must come from the minds and hearts of people.

Questioning Your Way to the Truth

Q: If I go sit for meditation and then meet with you at tea time to ask questions, will I get all my questions answered before I leave?

A: Some of your questions can be answered directly and immediately. Some in a roundabout way, for you need to contemplate and enter into them. And some I will completely ignore because you are not yet ready to hear the answer. Just because you form a question doesn't mean you can understand the answer. Some questions come merely from curiosity, not sincerity.

Q: On my way here I had some questions in mind that I wanted to ask you. But as I thought more about it, I started to have some doubts: maybe I should just try and think through the answers myself.

A: Yes, do that. If your questions are good questions, they will open the mind. When you turn your attention to the mind with the determination to observe it carefully, it responds by becoming softer and more flexible. This is the process that transforms adolescents into mature, caring adults.

But we must be aware of thought interfering in our investigation. We must discriminate between thinking and contemplation, for thought is a futile mode for studying profound spiritual questions. We must go beyond thought. This requires a jump into the unknown. When you are prepared to go it alone, holding on to nothing, you will go far beyond the limitations of thought, which keeps you in mental slavery. This is your spiritual destiny.

Q: I hope I'm not disturbing you. I expect that you must be tired of answering questions from naive visitors.

A: Answering questions about meditation practice is often energizing, so I don't find answering questions tedious. If the questioner is really sincere, there is a special, even holy, feeling in and around the conversation.

Of course, I am not so enthusiastic about answering stock questions about monks' undergarments and the shaving of our heads. But even those questions, I have now learned, have the potential to stimulate something deeper in the questioner. If I have the patience required to answer the questioner's needs rather than the question, then I am doing precisely what I should be doing in that moment. That is Dharma. Often what begins as curiosity develops into something more profound. Some day I hope to meet someone who will ask me, "Who is it that asks my questions?" Or, "What is there to seek?"

My own favorite question is this: "Who would I be if I let go of all the factors that make me think I am me? Would I be better off? Happier? If so, why?" Or, in another version: "Who am I when I don't think I am who I think I am?"

I came to practice meditation because I wanted to know the answers to a string of questions that I had been pursuing since childhood: Why are we here? What is goodness? Is there any value in goodness that an ordinary person—the sort who can be lured into foolish behavior—can make use of in this world? Why is the world as it is? Is there a God, and if so, can I depend upon him or her? What can I expect from an investment of faith in God, or, for that matter, an investment in cynicism?

Buddhist meditation is in no way daunted by these questions. The meditator contemplates these sorts of questions within the heart, going deeper and deeper into them with relentless determination. My own determination was so intense that I knew if I couldn't discover satisfactory answers, I would have to continue to search for a teaching that was powerful and wise enough to penetrate into and unravel these questions.

As it turned out, there wasn't any need to search further. I was amazed to find the answers were within myself, just as all spiritual teachings proclaim. Once I recognized the nature of the inner world, I knew that all I identified as my personal world, which caused so much grief and distress, spun out of the well of infinite consciousness. Everything I want and need to know is within me. I am within everything I need to know. Buddhist meditation has the tools that can access whatever I need to realize. There is a way to freedom.

PART TWO

Answers from the Forest

Your pain is the breaking of the shell that encloses your understanding.

—Kahlil Gibran

*C*onsider this: *only the attempt to escape suffering exceeds the magnitude of suffering.*

Most human enterprises, even the spiritual ones, are designed to transport us away from the experience of pain. Drugstores are continually expanding their inventory of painkillers for every kind of physical ailment; movie theaters, restaurants, and entertainment centers have proliferated to accommodate the faithful patrons who seek to ease the suffering of boredom and discontent; psychiatrists have a three-month waiting list for patient appointments; the 900 number for Psychic Connection has never been busier. We seek, we ask, and, still not finding the panacea for our pain, we seek some more, until the seeking itself becomes the suffering.

Then one day, we finally run out of places to go and things to do. Relief, after all, is not just a swallow away. Our heads bowed down in defeat and bitter disillusionment, we have nowhere else to look but inward. This is the moment when we are ready to learn; this is the time when the teacher appears.

Setting the Context for Practice

Q: I have been trying to simplify my life, but it just doesn't seem to work. I tried to live without a car, but it takes too much time to get around without one, so I decided to buy a old one. Occasionally there are good things on television, so I kept the TV. I have just about done away with furniture and now use a futon and mats that I can roll up. But I don't think I can reduce my things to the point where I don't have to pay much attention to them.

A: I gather you heard me talking to someone earlier about moving down the economic scale and reducing the number of material things in one's life. This is something everyone has to work out for him or herself. There is no sense in agonizing over the fact that you may still be attached to things you feel you should get rid of. Just let simplicity be a principle you value. At first you will simply be alert to not bringing more things into your home and into your life. Later, as you settle into this way of living, you will see the advantages of having less and will feel confident about letting go of things that you now still secretly cherish.

The main point of living simply is learning to be content with what you have. Most people experience little contentment in their lives. They always want more or better. In this age, simple living takes courage, strength of character, and discipline. The reward is a lightness of heart, a sense of freedom from the ever-wanting, perennially unsatisfied desiring that keeps people pre-occupied with things that are destined to perish.

I once asked a group of American teenagers what money cannot buy. They were stymied. No one could come up with an answer. Finally, I started offering some answers: time, good health, harmonious relationships, beauty, fresh air, clean water. They sat skeptically pondering these possibilities. Then I mentioned the two most important ones: silence and peace of mind.

They started refuting this list. They were convinced that money was the key to everything good—that money could bring you loyal friendships, provide you with beautiful surroundings, and even bring peace of mind, because financial prosperity could rid you of most worries.

I pointed out that rich people worry continuously about money; they are endlessly concerned with multiplying and pre-serving their wealth. Even if they had a money tree growing in their backyard, they would still worry about how to protect it.

I asked if anyone thought money could buy silence. No

one ventured a reply on that one. One boy agreed that silence is something money can't buy, but asked what's the point of it. Good health—well, money could provide you with higher quality food, which would make the body healthier. Fresh air, clean water—one could go backpacking or ride a mountain bike to where the air is clean and the water is safe to drink. As for a harmonious family life, wealth would certainly contribute to this.

These intelligent, typical middle-class teenagers were determined to refute almost anything I said that diminished the value of money. Anything that did not have a price tag, such as silence, had no value for them.

As the discussion drew to a close, I brought up something else that money cannot buy: spiritual experience. And yet this experience far surpasses any pleasure one could ever imagine, since it comes about when fear and desire are out of the way. Religious experience is to be discovered quite apart from concerns of money and material things. It is a refined sort of experience that rivets our attention and caresses our consciousness. Perhaps someday when they have learned the truth about the limitations of money, they might remember this conversation.

Q: I don't think anyone can deny that we need money to live in this world. My idea is that one should strive to become very rich. After that, there will be time and leisure enough to practice intensive meditation. You have proceeded this way, haven't you?

A: You haven't recognized that rich people need to devote themselves to their money. They have to guard it, administer it, and worry about how to make more money with it. Having money without wisdom means a life lived in an excruciating realm of hell.

It's better to establish yourself right from this moment in a moderate lifestyle in which you can keep your focus on spiritual development. Later on might be too late and you might have missed an opportunity.

I advocate this maxim: "Simplicity is sanity." Have just enough to live moderately in a way appropriate for householders. Keep in mind the words "good enough," rather than "more," "better," and "best." It's foolish to use the human mind only to think about wanting. For the most part, people who are ripe for spiritual practice have what they need in both material goods and experience.

Wanting and craving are paired with suffering and conflict. Contentment and simplicity are paired with wisdom. It is very important to live in a way that doesn't drive you crazy but rather drives you sane. You are driven sane by doing small, simple things carefully, thereby spiritualizing your activities. Live your life like a medicine man or woman.

Most of the desperate and neurotic suffering in the West comes from overabundance. Many of the heaviest sufferers are the people who have the most stuff. This is an ironic turn of events that wasn't expected to come along with the technological advancements of this age, which were supposed to make people happier. I understood this some years ago when I lived for six months in a tiny monastery on top of a mountain and found the circumstances far more ascetic than I had expected. Unlike most other monasteries in that part of Thailand, there wasn't much of anything available in the common storeroom—a few mosquito coils, batteries, and some light bulbs. I had just a few pieces of clothing, a recycled Pepsi bottle on a cord as a water bottle, and a fifty-cent pair of flip-flops that were just about flopped out. I remember that for two to three weeks I had just a few bits of candle that I would chop out of a large ceremonial candle to use in my hut. My match box was often too damp to ignite anything, so I learned to sit in the dark for much of the night.

Yet I was quite happy. Of course, there was still the human suffering that comes in any situation. Occasionally I was lonely and hungry, or felt despairing. But nothing was added onto that. I wasn't concerned that my match box might be stolen, and didn't need to worry whether my insurance covered recycled candles and second-hand flip-flops! There was a sense of peace that came with not having much of anything, and a sense of contentment from the satisfaction that I had what I needed. And since my needs were so simple, I felt at ease, confident that whatever I really needed would manifest. And it did.

Q: I'm still young and haven't decided what kind of career to pursue. The only thing I really know about myself is that I like to help people.

A: You are likely to find yourself doing social work of some kind. What is important, however, is not the particular field you study at the university, but your ability to center your life in what has meaning. If your life has meaning, it will develop toward something. Directing your life toward service to others is a noble and dignified way to live. But in order to have a real impact on others, you will first have to enrich your heart with purity, loving kindness, and compassion.

Make your field of study the development of noble inner qualities that you can bring into service to others.

Q: I have been living alone for some years and keep pretty much to myself. I sometimes wonder if I am selfish. Perhaps I should remarry and raise children.

A: To live alone and peacefully takes a certain talent, you know. It provides fewer opportunities to associate with fools—apart from the one in our own head! If you look at advertisements and go to theaters, you are invariably going to see people doing things as couples. "Couples are fun and singleness is lonely." However, some people—both lay persons and monks—including myself, enjoy aloneness and find it a productive lifestyle. Loneliness and aloneness are opposites.

If you want to help children grow into fine adults, you could volunteer your services through any one of many agencies and, thereby, help many more children than if you just have children of your own. The goodness rippling outward from your service will have considerable significance in this world, where selfishness has become the norm.

Q: I have decided not to meditate any more because it seems more important to develop computer skills.

A: You can choose to put all your energies in that direction. But if you become completely wired to the world, it will be at great expense. Computer people, in my experience, become alienated from reality. Not just distanced or confused, but alienated. This is tragic. It is like giving up a bag of gold for a pot of beans—the twenty-first-century version of that old folk tale. Computer nerds give up the unlimited potential of emptiness to become an isolated part of a pseudo-network. They buy into an abstract existence which people call virtual reality. Those who go in too deep lose all sense of what is natural. Be careful. I can see this from my own experience. I have written some things on a computer—and that machine had no Internet, CD, or game capacity!

The environment we choose to live in—our home, our friends, our intimate partners—has tremendous influence on the way we live and the direction our life is moving. It is critical to our well-being. We can live comfortably and safely in a dead and dried-out, riskless situation in which we are prompted only to entertain ourselves with frivolous activities. Or, we can choose to live in a vibrant, challenging environment, which however obliges us to live with a degree of uncertainty. Moving out farther toward the edge, where things are not so much in our control and we are forced to explore the unknown, provokes the body and mind to be vigilant and awake.

To live in this manner is not to deliberately seek out life-threatening circumstances, such as living in slums. In such places we are forced to use all our mental energy just to survive. Prisons, for instance, are very difficult places for a person to grow; even though a prisoner has few duties and a lot of time on his hands, the need to protect himself from others predominates. It is difficult to turn within. It is difficult to find like-minded, spiritually oriented friends.

If we have good spiritual companions, friends who support and encourage us to grow in a good way, we can live just about anywhere. We feel confident, and our practice progresses. Once our practice is strong, a difficult environment becomes a challenge instead of an obstacle.

Beginning Practice

Q: What is the ultimate objective of a Buddhist?

A: To respond to the world like a Buddha.

Q: And how is that?

A: With affectionate and intelligent understanding—a sympathetic understanding of the struggle required to disentangle ourselves, the kind of all-embracing compassion that a mother holds for her only child.

Q: How does one come to that state?

A: By becoming disenchanted with the things that wise people become disenchanted with. Or, we can say, by becoming one who has become unstuck from everything sticky in the world;

from everything the mind and body can get stuck into.

Q: Isn't that just about everything?

A: Now you get the point.

Q: (*Three days later, the same person . . .*) I have been thinking about all the things in our culture that I "get stuck into," to
use your expression. It is a long list, but not so long that it covers
everything, as you imply. I wonder if I'm still missing the point.

A: It's good that you followed up our conversation with
contemplation. I don't know what items you noted on your list,
but I strongly suspect that they include sensual items like food,
music, sex, entertainment, computer games, pleasant aromas, and
things of that kind. The influence of these sense-pleasing items is
very apparent. But there is a deeper, more subtle level of stickiness
that is usually hidden from our understanding.

Q: Such as . . . ?

A: Our cherished views and opinions, the secret hopes we
harbor, our hidden guilt, our fantasies. These are all created out of
thin air, for none of them are real, nor do they belong to anyone.
Bubbles, that's all they are, just soap bubbles. And yet they exert a
tremendous pressure over our lives. They keep us spinning endlessly. The mind embraces these notions and becomes shackled to
them. They anchor the mind to the bottom of the ocean of life.

Q: How does one escape from them?

A: Through meditation practice. Make an effort to recognize those energies that confine and limit our lives. Isolate them. Sand them down. File them down. Chisel them down one chip at a time, day by day. Keep observing everything with careful scrutiny—everything, including the observer. Shake every concept loose until nothing is left of what you previously mistook for something.

When the mind is empty of both coarse and subtle things, it enters into the stream of life free. From then on you can just flow effortlessly with the energy of life, secure in the realization of the way things are.

Life is a challenge. There is an art to living it well. And, like any art, diligent training is required to do it skillfully. The sooner we learn the ropes, the smoother the ride. The choice whether to live foolishly or skillfully lies entirely within the range of each person's power. There are other things beyond this range that we can't begin to control. If we are clever, we keep our nose out of those aspects of our life and turn toward what we can control, alter, improve, and transform.

It is obvious that each person is obliged to live his or her own life and take responsibility for all life choices and decisions. No one can bear the responsibility for our actions but ourselves. Life doesn't allow us to bury our heads in the sand to escape this. Nor does it make sense to kick the wall and protest against the misinformed perception that life is not fair. And "couch-potatoing out" is not an option on the menu. We are obliged to meet and embrace our life. If we can do this with grace and dignity, our life blossoms. If we don't, life sinks deeply into the emotional and psychological potholes of guilt, apathy, and cynicism, which lead to addictions and depression. Nature demands that we grow, otherwise, we become stagnant. There is an inner directive that calls us to be who we are, to manifest our destiny. That being the case, we would be wise to move into our lives with intelligence, with courage, and with the enthusiastic interest necessary to develop our skills for living. Directing our life thus absolutely prevents it from withering into a tangle of remorse and regret.

It is our duty to find the time and space, no matter how cramped and difficult our circumstances may be, to outgrow our immaturity and grow into our inherent loveliness. In this way we incline our life toward wisdom and compassion. By beginning at the beginning, performing small gestures of warm-hearted concern for others, we pave the way for a time when we will be able to squeeze a great deal of kindness into any situation. In this way we can help bring peace into the world.

The most appropriate place to start is in our home. In small ways. And continuously, so that a pattern begins to emerge and old perceptions fade away. This is easier said than done, but it can be done. If the vision of a life brought into balance and harmony is kept in mind, this all becomes possible. The vision of bringing light and love into our home is a powerful impetus for evolutionary change. With this in mind we can endeavor to be a force for bringing harmony to our home. We can work to be willing to let go of everything that puts us in conflict with others. This is a beautiful gesture. This is the skill and art needed to live in our world in an elegant way; one that amplifies goodness rather than weighs the world down by decreasing goodness.

Often the best thing to do—the wise and humble response—in a difficult situation at home or anywhere is to leave the scene and enter into silence. We die to the inner fool, the clown who would act recklessly and say things that bite deeply. Learning to choose the path of a wise person in difficult situations develops the ability to act intelligently when overwhelming situations arise and threaten to blow us away into confusion.

If we have a meditative glimpse into the nature of time, we know that this moment is all there ever is. The future grows out of this very moment. Each of us, as beings conditioned by karma, carries the whole of a past we don't even remember in an energy stream we cannot see. We know intuitively that habits, patterns, proclivities, attitudes, and the like are deeply embedded. Only a bit of all this can we connect to the experiences in our present life. The rest is unknown, an enigma. If karma is a reality—and cutting-edge science is now ready to concede that it is—then certainly life will continue to present an almost endless sequence of challenges that prompt contemplation and reflection for the seeker. If we meet life with wisdom and compassion, further problems won't come tumbling out of our actions. Rather, we will recognize life as a flow of changing circumstances and meet it accordingly.

Q: I think I need a beeper to wake me up every three minutes, or some sort of electric device to wear on my wrist that would give me a little jolt. Has anyone ever tried this high-tech method of staying alert?

A: To begin with, every three minutes wouldn't be often enough. If you recognize the need for a little bit of alertness, you must see that what is needed is a continuous, twenty-four-hour-a-day, seven-days-a-week awareness of who you are.

The awareness you seek must come from inside, supported by ethics and morality. This awareness prompts us to be here and now, in the present moment. This then leads to *samadhi,* or concentration, which in turn will awaken your dormant wisdom-compassion. This is a thumbnail sketch of the path to awakening.

Attitude is the key to the whole enterprise of meditation. It is the take-off point where all the other factors in a meditative life begin. If our attitude runs off track in one particular direction, we will find ourselves off in that direction for quite some time—just as in long-distance air travel, a few degrees make the difference between arriving in Iraq or in Thailand. Therefore, the serious meditator is obliged to be super-vigilant about attitude.

A clear, balanced attitude—one that does not cause mischief, that is settled and neutral, that recognizes that a meditative life is lived in the conventional world—is a great asset. All that we do, all our efforts to make headway in spiritual practice, are subject to patterns of our life that operate automatically—some would say diabolically—and entrap us. Not knowing that this is the prevailing condition, there is no possibility of recognizing an escape route even if we stumbled into one. We are like the blind turtle that fell into a mine shaft: there is no possibility of an exit. The machinery of thought that we have become chained to leads us by the nose again and again down the darkened path of familiarity. And the most familiar message we hear is the one which tells us we are who we think we are.

A clear, balanced attitude, which we can call an intelligent attitude, makes it possible to sidestep this deception. It maintains the awareness that things are not as they seem, that we are not who we think we are, that there are dimensions beyond our present level of consciousness toward which we can incline ourselves. An intelligent attitude has confidence that enlightenment is possible. It brings sufficient energy into our practice. There is nothing fixed that we have to surrender to. Our future is in our own hands.

An intelligent attitude is the key to setting aside the naivete that people sometimes bring to their practice. Just as an archer has calculated in the back of his mind for the wind factor as he aims for the target, so the intelligent seeker can proceed confidently and with clarity, knowing that he or she must practice within the framework of the mind, which is a world of deceptions, doubts, and temptations. An intelligent attitude has the savvy to use skillful means, acquired over lifetimes, to let go of the sticky conditions that try to keep us mired. We are able to sit above the world, not be embedded in it. There is a space where we can be clear and uninvolved. It is this sliver of non-involvement with the mind's machinations that allows us to remain unstuck to anything that arises.

Right attitude creates a space from where we can gain a foothold beyond the mind. A right attitude has been dipped into the nectar of awareness and so will not be led astray for long. When our meditative consciousness has this courage and clarity, it is able to go against the grain and break the hold of conventional behavior and thinking. A seed sprouts, the seed of trans-sensibility—an evolved consciousness that recognizes two dimensions of experience almost simultaneously. We can be aware of both the object of observation as well as the detached observer. This in itself is already transformative.

There is a further dimension in which the meditator is not an object of awareness and there is no object of meditation. There is only an awareness, far more subtle, that isn't involved with anything—no doing, no thinking, no creating. Here the ball and chain that connect us to the sense of personality are severed, at least for a while. This is the peace that all seekers aspire to—not merely the peace of a temporary internal quietude, but a peace beyond the reach of thought—the true peace of mind.

Q: Don't you find walking the path to enlightenment hard?

A: Difficult, of course. There were times in the course of intensive mind training when I thought my mind would explode from the conflict of inner forces, or that I would burst into a hysterical, unstoppable crying fit. Something inside of me knew that if I didn't grit my teeth and hold firmly to my faith in the Buddha-Dharma, I would fall deeper into the predicament that spins my life as it does. Living through those moments of crisis, the word *difficulty* enlarged to describe a greater magnitude of existential pain.

There are periods in the lives of all of us who aspire to do good and progress along the path when we have to be satisfied with just being able to squeak by and survive an onslaught of karmic conditions. There are times when difficulty is so permeated by sorrow that we can only lock the door and cry into our pillow. Then, as it must, it changes.

Q: Are you saying that this level of psychological pain or suffering was more than you were willing to confront?

A: Yes. It was almost to the point of saying if to practice mental training one has to face this level of conflict and suffering, I will look somewhere else for my spiritual needs.

Q: That kind of suffering puts me off.

A: You are quick to be put off. You throw in the towel before you consider the benefits that come from noble aspiration and determined practice. If you don't accept that all spiritual growth involves hard work, going against the grain, enduring what you would prefer to avoid, then I don't think I can be of much help to you.

You could look around trying to find a namby-pamby teaching vehicle that won't challenge you or demand anything from you. If you find such a thing, go for it! Good luck! But I don't think it will take you where you truly want to go. You have to remember that whatever you do, wherever you go, you go there and do that with your mind as it is.

Suffering is essential to gaining wisdom. Suffering needs to know why there is suffering. Invariably, the universe answers: "Things are as they are." We can argue that they shouldn't be so, but the universe replies: "If they shouldn't be, they wouldn't be."

When there is a gulf between our notion of what we want the world to be and what the world is, what we want the world to be has to either bend or break. In the humility of this understanding we can restructure our life in a way that accords with reality.

As a working hypothesis you can bring to your practice the notion that the problem generating human suffering is well disguised and that it will require a great deal of determined effort and clever methodology to discover it and root it out.

The problem is well disguised because it is enclosed and protected by our most cherished belief: that we exist as we think we do. This notion has become a habit pattern so tightly held onto that only a few rare, wise beings have come to recognize it for what it is. Somehow, in some way, we have to step back from this notion. Our best ally and the only force that can unveil the delusion and bring things into clarity is wisdom. Wisdom supersedes the enchantment that surrounds and enhances the illusion of who we think we are.

When you sit in meditation, reflect upon this predicament. Then your practice will have benefits beyond mere relaxation. Or, it will become true relaxation, which means moving away from the influence of what leads us astray. Your practice will be protected from becoming another mindless habit. We must endeavor to maintain the alertness that makes our meditation a kind of magical unfolding, an adventure that frees the heart and leads us to grace.

Chapter Three

The Buddhist Tradition

Q: I believe, as one famous teacher has proclaimed, that truth is a pathless land and that all forms of rituals and conventions that come with orthodox religions just weigh the truth down and keep it in the mundane. For this reason, even though Buddhist ideology strongly appeals to me, it is a path I steer away from.

A: Do you steer away from other religions as well?

Q: Indeed.

A: Where has all this determined steering gotten you? Are you free? Are you on your way to freedom? Or at least can you say you are now committed to a practice that turns you away from the negative patterns of living that entangle and enslave you? In short, are you becoming freed up?

Q: No, I can't truthfully say that I'm becoming freed up.

A: Then maybe something critical is missing. I don't doubt your interest or sincerity, but I have noticed other intelligent people like yourself who want to overlook the ground-level aspects of spiritual development. You are just too high-minded, too idealistic. Don't we need a ground to build upon? In your hypothesis, where is the ground from which you can attain what you aspire to?

We just don't wake up to the truth of the nature of the universe. In fact, if this realization occurred suddenly, with no foundation and preparation, we wouldn't be able to be with it. Truth arises through a disciplined practice that is grounded in the factors that incubate spiritual development, that moves step by step from level to level. We grow from coarse to subtle, from external to internal, from material to immaterial, from form to formless.

So we need to begin with external symbols. We can choose an appropriate symbol, one that is in harmony with our aspiration. For instance, we might regard a Buddha statue as a beautiful artifact embodying compassion, stillness, and wisdom. We do this not out of superstition or to follow a cultural norm; that would indeed just bog us down in the mundane. We must see through a spiritual symbol to see what it actually stands for deep in our heart.

The same is true with rituals. We don't engage in rituals in order to further darken the clouds of delusion that appear between us and the ultimate reality. Rituals are what we make of them. Every seeker must recognize that an external form is merely that—an external form—while the home of the heart is the inner world. Imbue forms and rituals with deep meaning, and they will lead you toward the pathless land, the inner reality where enlightenment blossoms.

Q: I am a person who doesn't believe in religion at all. Period. Some people say Buddhism is a philosophy, others say it is a religion. Still others call it a way of life. I haven't decided what to call it. But this meditation that is being taught by monks and nuns seems to me an irrational religious activity.

A: I suppose you can see it that way. But why not just use it as a tool, without trying to dissect it to fit your belief system? Simply practice meditation in order to live a better life, or even just to live a good life, whatever meaning that holds for you. Or, meditate as a means of learning how not to be afraid—of death, or of all the insignificant concerns that paralyze your innate ability to live fully. Meditate to activate creativity. Meditate to recognize the value of the truly good things in life: friendship, honor, respect, compassion, and love.

Meditation accesses the subconscious energy that brings divergent energies into harmony. It lifts us above our sense of self, with its kaleidoscope of apparent needs. This ordinary realm is so dense with suffering that we forget to get out of the way and give ourselves to the appropriateness of the moment.

Q: I have a problem with bowing to Buddha images in the meditation hall. I don't feel comfortable doing it.

A: You don't have to bow at all. The images are there for your benefit, not to intimidate you. They are not sitting there waiting to be bowed to. No one is making a video of you bowing to graven images to send to your mother!

If you find these representations helpful for recollecting a way of being, then you should make use of them as such. If you find that they bring up aversion in you, you should make use of them as such. This is a path of wisdom. You are being encouraged to bring wisdom to the present moment in order to see things as they are.

You could practice bowing in private toward a mirror. See what that situation does for you. How does it feel? Do you feel foolish? Do you feel that it is purely a superstitious gesture? See for yourself.

Q: Being a religion that encourages direct experience over belief, is there a place for faith in Buddhism?

A: Faith is reckoned as one of the spiritual powers in Buddhism, but it is faith based on reason rather than blind faith. The teachings of the Buddha are to be investigated and reflected upon until one understands their meaning, depth, and value. Then, when one puts these teachings to the test by practicing them and experiencing their results, one finds that genuine faith nourishes virtue, awareness, wisdom, and liberation.

In Buddhism, as in other religions, certain basic tenets are accepted on faith. One of these is the relation between cause and effect, especially concerning wholesome and unwholesome actions and their results. The Christian counterpart of this teaching is: "You reap what you sow."

For one who has not yet experienced the fruits of Dharma practice, faith is essential. For some, faith manifests intuitively from walking the Buddhist path and finding that the teachings are worthy of trust.

Q: How do Buddhists believe the world was created?

A: The Buddha purposely steered way from this enigmatic, mind-boggling question. He said that conjecture about creation could so dominate and fascinate the mind that, eventually, the struggle to know what is unknowable would flip the mind and one would go mad. Scientists, of course, don't go over the top with their cool, rational observations, but they run with their proliferating thoughts until they can't return to balance again.

How the world was created, if it was created at all, is unthinkable. My intuition strongly suggests that it wasn't created in any sense we can understand. It is as it always is. This makes understanding it a dilemma of a far greater order than any Western scientific hypothesis can possibly address.

Q: What do you call God?

A: God—that word is too loaded to deal with.

Q: But how do you describe God?

A: To try to describe God is to walk blindly and arrogantly into quicksand. If you must have an answer, call it Nature.

Q: And what is Nature?

A: The wise will leave it at that.

Q: I've read quite a few books on Buddhism and have always felt uplifted and inspired by them. Last summer I visited several other Buddhist countries in Southeast Asia and was totally inspired by the Buddhists I met there. However, here in Thailand I become disillusioned when I visit the Buddhist monasteries. Is Buddhism dead? Is Buddhism dying? I don't see any connection between the morally and ethically exalted teachings I read in the books and the superficial, lethargic sense I get when I visit most monasteries.

A: The absurdity of this age has infected and infiltrated the monasteries here just as it has the monasteries and churches abroad. Still, there are a few islands or pockets where the exalted teachings you have been reading are being lived. A few, not many.

Yes, Buddhism is dying in some places. But it is alive and well in a few remote monasteries throughout Asia. What you have been observing is merely the peel of a delectable fruit, or the outer shell of a pearl-laden oyster. None of that is truly representative of the Buddha's teachings. This exterior is the fringes of popular tradition mixed up with local custom. True religious teaching is always in conflict with superstition. But superstition, because it offers a quick fix to the problems and anxieties of life, is always popular with the majority of people.

The rise and decline of Buddhism is not a unique story. It is the-way-things-are. You can rest assured that Buddhism in its original and pure form is still practiced and that it is available to anyone ready to make use of it. This is an incredible blessing.

Q: I know that in some Buddhist countries belief in ghosts is very prevalent. Do the teachings of Buddhism include belief in such spirits?

A: The belief in ghosts in Asian culture is very deep and broad. The mainstream cultures and the subcultures have names for all the various species of ghosts that inhabit cremation grounds, hospitals, trees, forests, and such. Movies commonly feature ghost themes and stories.

It wasn't so long ago that the people of northeast Thailand believed that demons and unfriendly spirits lurked everywhere, waiting for a chance to kill their livestock, or worse still, their children. They would frequently offer food on their farmland and in the surrounding forests to appease ravenous spirits. They sought protective charms and amulets from holy recluses, who they believed had some kind of power over these spirits. They would give unattractive nicknames to their children, such as "mangy dog," "gecko," "snake," "stinky," and so on, hoping to deceive the evil spirits into believing that their children were not worth devouring.

It wasn't until the forest monks established their monasteries in the region that the people's way of thinking began to incline toward Dharma, and their superstitious beliefs started to wane. Their greatest fears—darkness and death—gradually gave way to an understanding of the-way-things-are. The days of wailing and desperate mourning of their dead have been replaced with a more appropriate sadness and affectionate remembrance of the deceased loved one, and then life goes on as before. This is an example of how a community benefits from the wisdom teachings of the holy men and women whom it supports.

CHAPTER FOUR

A Foundation in Ethics

Q: Why are ethics and morality stressed so strongly in Theravada Buddhism?

A: The Buddha himself taught that ethics and morality are the first step. Without these as the foundation, concentration and wisdom—the insight and realization we are seeking—cannot arise. As long as there are activities of body, speech, or mind that cause agitation and disharmony, there will be too much confusion and too many negative emotions for the mind to be clear. The spin of all this confusion is just too disabling for true awareness to be reached.

Living morally is very simple for some people and very, very difficult for others. It all depends on the assets of goodness and kindness stored within a person's karma.

Morality and ethics are just the beginning. Nonetheless, some of us need to spend most of our lifetime just putting down strong moral roots. Once these are established and strong, we begin to see the mind as it is.

How beneficial it would be if there were a bold revival in the sphere of education, emphasizing polite behavior and holding graceful etiquette as worthy as skills in sports. If children had a value for respectful behavior, they would understand that many people in their lives are worthy of respect: their parents, who look after them; their teachers, who work everyday to give them the opportunity to learn about the world they have been born into. They would come to understand that virtue itself is worthy of respect and that goodness is universally recognized as an attribute of a fine human being.

I remember seeing important generals come to visit venerated monks. They would come to the foyer of the monk's dwelling and take off their super-shiny shoes, and unfasten their gun belts and lay them next to their shoes. Their bodyguards would follow them, putting down all their paraphernalia of combat and taking off their boots. They would all enter the receiving area together and bow gracefully to the monk and the statue of the Buddha. Some of them bowed as gracefully as ballet dancers.

After their talk with the monk, they would take their leave, bowing reverently once again before finally leaving the room. Outside the hut they would put back on their small arsenal of arms and ammunition and go about their business, refreshed and humbled. Bowing and graceful behavior played an important part in that transformation.

Q: In Buddhism are the standards of morality the same for everyone? For example, is a Buddhist soldier asked to refrain from killing, drinking alcohol, and visiting brothels?

A: Here in Thailand, we teach commercial fishermen not to kill other human beings. If we taught them that they should not kill anything, the teaching would have no value for them. It would set a standard they could not live up to. These people have this sort of unfortunate karma to bear. They are not at a level of karma where they are able to make more refined moral choices. Since childhood they have fished, drunk alcohol, smoked cigarettes, and squabbled among themselves over petty concerns. They have a hard time not killing one another.

This is an example of the relativity of things. Situations and karma vary dramatically from person to person.

Sexuality is another example that is quite relevant these days. A person with a sexual addiction most likely has a difficult time being discriminative regarding partners. While the best practice is sexual monogamy, this standard would be out of reach for a person with a sexual addiction problem. So instead, the best spiritual advice would be to refrain from exploitative sex, such as sex with minors or with people already committed to another relationship. And, just as important, to try not to exploit one's own body. We all have to begin where we are. Spiritual guidance is flexible and must be adjusted to each person's personal dilemmas. Here wisdom supercedes inflexible moral precepts.

Q: A lot of teaching in Theravada Buddhism is centered on morality, whereas the Buddha, if I understand rightly, said that in regards to morality one could cut right through everything extraneous and just rely upon wisdom in all our conduct. This sounds like the core of this aspect of the teaching.

A: I can appreciate the hope and desire behind your question. This is an important point that does need to be understood properly.

The basic teaching regarding morality and ethics is not meant to be a straitjacket as much as it is intended to be a leash—something to keep us from going too far astray and getting into mischief. Morality is essential as the foundation for the development of concentration. When concentration arises, wisdom naturally follows.

Clever people can be quite cunning in their attempts to completely bypass precepts and guidelines. For instance, one can say that in deciding to follow the precepts there must already be some underlying wisdom present in the heart. Otherwise, what would prompt us to want to restrain and refine our behavior? What, apart from wisdom, prompts us to stop running in circles and chasing our tail? So, arguably, wisdom is already functioning right from the start.

We need to be clear that this wisdom isn't the Buddha's wisdom, the ultimate truth. Rather, we can call this preliminary level of wisdom a kind of clear faith. It is a wisdom that still involves thinking—a clever, calculated kind of wisdom.

The Buddha's wisdom is the wisdom of Emptiness. It arises by stages and has its foundation in morality. It is outside the domain of thought. You can't think it out. It You need to study your mind through meditation in order to know anything about Emptiness.

How can you know or appreciate the profundity of Emptiness until you have walked a part of the path? When a glimmer of Emptiness arises in the mind of someone who has yet to do this work, it is disregarded as strange and of no consequence.

I know from my own experience the desire to seek and take shortcuts. But if you do, you're likely to flounder from lack of confidence as soon as the going gets choppy. Better to follow the footsteps of the enlightened ones.

Q: What is selfishness?

A: Selfishness is the response that puts ME first. Selfishness bulls its way ahead of events. It is concerned not with what the situation calls for, but with putting ME first. The more you observe selfishness, the more you see that it is always off track and out of tune. If we want to get it right, we need to attune ourselves to act in a "me last" mode. All life is a test to see if we have learned to maintain this "me last" in all situations.

It is also true that people do good deeds in order to get something for themselves. These acts, good as they are, are diminished in their worth because they are tainted by the stench of self. Still, doing them is better than not doing them. The highest motive for doing good is simply to do good for its own sake. For in not seeking anything in return, one opens oneself to the greatest merits and deepest joys that come with selfless deeds.

Freedom is the absence of selfishness; it is selflessness.

Q: Suppose someone who has lived a dissolute and foolish life suddenly has an insight into the value of morality, and then turns herself completely around and ends up embracing the five Buddhist precepts. Is this person morally better and stronger than someone who has always kept the five precepts faithfully? Is there more merit in making such a radical transformation?

A: In Buddhist circles, everyone who keeps the precepts is considered equal, as they have all risen to the level of a true human being. However, someone who has undergone a spiritual transformation such as you are talking about would have considerable momentum and confidence going for her. She should parlay this energy by developing *samadhi,* or concentration. This will come easily for someone who has settled into an ethical and moral lifestyle. Worry and anxiety won't disturb her mind. Once sufficient concentration is developed, the meditator can make her escape.

Q: In Buddhism, what do you mean by compassion?

A: That is a great question. It opens the way for insight into the essence of the Buddha's teaching.

Compassion is the gut feeling that all other creatures are essentially the same as we are. All sentient beings are one because all of us share the same fate—old age, illness, and death. This is an inescapable, painful cycle, and the compassionate heart feels empathy.

In meditation practice we deepen and enlarge this understanding until we become the compassionate heart. This becomes our mood and our attitude in all our interpersonal relationships.

If you contemplate this, you will see that compassion is the warmth that displaces anger, ill-will, jealousy, hatred, greed, lust, and fear of other beings. It is very different from sympathy, which involves a sense of superiority and the presence of a dominating I-Ego.

CHAPTER FIVE

The Illusion of Self

Q: What kind of person does Buddhism try to help its followers become?

A: No kind of person.

Q: What I mean is, what does a Buddhist try to become?

A: Pure being. When we abide in who we truly are, we shift into the peaceful, effortless state that is not involved with conflict.

Q: What is the biggest obstacle to spiritual development?

A: The biggest obstacle, of course, is the illusion of the I-Ego, which manifests itself in many ways. The common thread among them all is that they are troublesome. Each comes with an attached energy-pack of unskillful tendencies that exert enormous influence upon us. These, along with a pattern of embedded habits, are what get us into all sorts of regrettable mischief and keep us running around in the same circles.

The I-Ego is the major villain in the drama of our lives. The irony is that we have to discover and diligently practice skillful means in order to circumvent something that we come to realize never existed in the first place.

Several decades ago in Berkeley, California—of course—there was a spoof campaign for president of the United States. The candidate was Mr. Nobody. The campaign slogan was "Nobody for President." A ticker-tape parade was organized and a convertible limousine was hired for the occasion. Motorcycle police flanked the automobile as it made its way down the main boulevard. Nobody was in the back seat.

At the time, that event was a definitive moment in my appreciation of American politics. Looking back, I now recognize that it was also a powerful demonstration of the reality of our human condition. There is no one in the back, or the front, seat.

There is a chain of assumptions that creates the image of the physical body as solid and permanent. This is an illusion. The sense organs also miss the boat. They tell us that the life process is continuous and stable. But it is not so. This body is in fact dissolving and reforming in the smallest units of change possible from one micro-moment to the next. Formation—dissolution—formation—dissolution continuously, until the body finally loses the ability to attract and hold the four elements that comprise it, and the karmic energy expires. The body is merely a meeting point where the elements congregate for a brief period of time.

Because there is dissolution and reformation, there must necessarily be empty or free space. Space exists on either side of a micro-moment of formation as it comes into being and dissolves again. So there is actually twice as much space as there is formation. Here is a quantitative expression of the reality of emptiness.

In conventional life we emphasize the formation phase, the micro-moments that create a field of tremendous, unstoppable activity. In Dharma we emphasize the space before and after, which is the more prevalent reality by at least two to one.

Honing in on what is factually the reality, we aren't going to be so inclined to grasp onto things that are not here more often than they're here. Life cools down, slows down, and deepens because there is no one to be worried about. No one is ever there.

Q: Do memories fade away? Though I am now able to refrain from most of the stupid escapades of my youth, some of the more exciting and sensual memories come around in my meditation and pounce on me. What can I do to escape these reruns?

A: If you skillfully practice letting go of all notions of self, you will find that these memories have no place to attach themselves to. The sense of self keeps reinforcing the idea of you as a consistent, constant, continuous entity. Memories are built upon and confirmed by this notion. But you are not the personality you think yourself to be. Through practice you come to recognize that you are a composite of changing conditions that have temporarily amassed into the form you regard yourself to be. In Dharma language, you are merely a karmic condition; you arise and pass away under the dictates of karma. The emotional energy connected to your memories draws you in because you continuously consent to being who you think you are.

If you cut yourself off from this misperception, you will cease to exist in a way that memory can bother you. If you are not really who you think you are, then memories are just old karmic images. Memory then has nowhere to hang its hat.

Q: I want to know what it would be like to be an *arahant,* an enlightened being. To become one is why I became a monk.

A: I hope you attain that noble aspiration. But I can tell you that when you arrive at your goal, you will find that there is *no one* to experience anything. I'm not saying that I know this from my own accomplishment. But I can say that I understand this from my experience in meditation and from a realization, through deep contemplation, of the nature of enlightenment. Enlightenment is a non-emotional, non-reflective way of being, a floating along, untouched by the world. Unburdened and unencumbered, the enlightened mind abides in absolute freedom. It is constantly alert and responsive in every way. The *arahant* lives in peace, harmlessly and harmoniously.

Having attained this transcendent reality, there is no one in him who would want to write home about his life as an *arahant!*

Chapter Six

Managing the Mind

Q: What should I do with all the crazy, demeaning, and perverted thoughts that come through my mind?

A: If these thoughts were yours, no one would dare to be within ten miles of you! They are not. They are just passing through. All people without exception, be they war criminals of the worst kind or exemplary individuals like Mother Teresa and the Dalai Lama, are subject to unworthy thoughts. You have been around for who-knows-how-many lifetimes—something you may not believe—and in this lifetime alone you have watched hundreds of movies and been bombarded with thousands of images on television. It's not surprising that these merge with each other and at some point produce horrific scenes in your mind. Just recognize that all these are not yours. If they were, you would be able to control them. But you can't. Just know that they only make their appearance in your mind. One of the great blessings of meditation practice is to see that the mind-stuff is not ours. Therefore, it is foolish to feel guilty, fearful, or even uneasy about what takes place in your mind. You are not your mind; you are much more.

The wise and holy people in this world are worthy of great respect precisely because they are no longer vulnerable to thoughts similar to the ones that taunt you.

The mind runs about hunting for things on which thoughts can proliferate. It thinks, creates, and weaves fantasies because that is its nature. But we also have the choice of letting the fantasies go. The ability to discern and let go is a function of the wisdom-compassion that is always present in one who cultivates a spiritual life.

Some of us purposely harbor distracting thoughts—sexual fantasies, romantic adventure fantasies, fantasies of power, and so on. When we understand the nature of the mind and the path of practice toward enlightenment, we stop playing with such thoughts and let go of them as swiftly as they arise. Soon they lose ground and fade away.

Q: I feel "freaked-out" almost all the time. I think you know what I mean. My mind flits between despair, disgust, anxiety, and guilt. This, mind you, is my normal state. I think drugs must be the path for my kind of mind.

A: Don't be ridiculous. This is the way most people's minds are. Only they live such busy, outwardly oriented lives that these mental states are suppressed and remain hidden. If we took the "doing" out of their lives, what would be left? The kinds of mental states you are experiencing.

You have a discerning intellect to be able to observe these states of mind. You are already more than halfway home in recognizing the importance of moods and contemplating their volatile nature. Now, go deeper and see what is behind them. You will find that there is nothing to them and that change is the nature of the backdrop.

Like most people, you would like to see your spiritual life unfold in a series of warm, joyful, and pleasant experiences—a step-by-step junket through spiritual Disney Worlds and Expos. But the process is both more sober and more sublime than that. Diligently work with your object of meditation day and night. Make your meditation your priority. Don't judge yourself or evaluate your life experiences in terms of fun and pleasure only. Be one who can endure what others would seek to obscure.

Q: Do you think that psychoanalysis is useful as an adjunct to meditation?

A: If therapy can stimulate profound questions about the nature of life itself, it can be a useful vehicle.

In the beginning, analysis will stimulate questions about the self. The client can contemplate what it is to be a "self" and ponder the problems it has caused. If the therapist is competent, he or she can help the client learn a lot about how the personality or self came to be as one perceives it to be.

In my experience as a client, a meditator, and a teacher, I have observed that focusing on the I-Ego benefits a person who has never before stopped to consider his or her life very carefully. If, in addition, that person learns to observe the process of inquiry itself, with all its doubts, worries, exaggerated concerns, and anxieties, then the person has advanced to the point of reflecting on thought and the patterns of thought.

If this process of careful introspection leads to an investigation of the nature of the self, the whole exercise of analysis will have yielded great benefit. The client will have some inkling of the machinations of the ego and will have begun to question and contemplate life to the point of turning toward an introspection into life itself. And in the end the client will have developed some skills and sufficient confidence to question the validity of the self, realizing how the self, with all its misguided desires, seeks out objects to stick onto with the inevitable result—acute suffering. This is the pain that led to therapy in the first place. In this way therapy can lead to contemplation and meditation.

Our way of seeing things has become distorted to the point where we must seek out therapies to encourage the mind to return to the balanced centeredness that makes for sanity.

Every wise teacher I have known has wholeheartedly endorsed moral discipline as the ethical fence surrounding one's spiritual growth. Moral discipline establishes reasonable and sensitive boundaries for one's behavior. In these stable conditions development can proceed; we can nurture our spiritual development and become better at the art of living, the art of meeting our karma head on.

However, when we attempt to deal with our life's challenges, we encounter the insidious and frustrating fact that our greatest challenges cannot be solved at the same psychological level where they manifest as problems. We must have a tool—a therapy or a teaching—that elevates us above the confusion of our personal world.

We enhance our spiritual life by incorporating and integrating what we learn along the way, and each lesson becomes part of the foundation for the next. As our understanding evolves, we continue using skillful tools and therapies to uplift us further, and so we are continuously growing beyond ourselves.

Q: I suffer from intense pangs of anguish when I have to choose between things.

A: You suffer from doubt. Doubt deceives us into believing that something is better than something else—and then it pulls the rug out from under that choice and makes it appear that the other choice is better! You could expend all your mental energy just jumping back and forth between alternatives. Everyone except an enlightened being suffers from this difficult fetter. A fetter that affects our mind more than our behavior is difficult to see.

Doubt is one of the more slippery ones. If we have the type of mind that is vulnerable to it yet doesn't understand it, it can just about drive us crazy.

With meditation practice we can come to understand the tricks involved in doubt and get out of its grasp. If you look carefully at doubt you will see that fear is part of it as well. Perhaps you see just a little fear wedged in with the doubt, but that little bit is just the tip of an iceberg, for where a little bit of fear is showing, there is certainly a lot more hidden behind it.

Whenever you notice doubt arising, study the mind. Until you can manage doubt, you can hold on to the understanding that whatever choice we make, an opportunity or field for learning inevitably comes along with it. Any choice is okay if we approach it with this attitude. We make the best choice we can and then examine our choice, observing its effects and integrating that learning into our life experience.

Q: In my meditation I keep running into a painful sequence of memories that seems to replay itself at will. It seems I have to just be there and take it all, without consent or control. What can I do to stop this?

A: Understand what a memory is. When we understand anything, that thing loses its power. On the other hand, by not knowing and by looking away in aversion, the thing retains its potency and continues to be threatening because there is fear.

What you can do is dislodge the memory's sacredness. Accept it as something presently painful but also changing. Contemplate the painful part. See how you can loosen the grip of time in this respect. These memories are flashbacks of images caught in time. You, the observer, are really only here in the present. The images of the past don't belong to you. They are analogue rather than reality.

Through meditation practice we are able to look into the source of things. Examining the question "What is a memory built upon?" we come to know what memory is from the bottom up. It can then no longer disturb the mind. Understanding that memories are merely mental constructs strips them of power.

It takes some courage to work through this. If you spend some time and effort on it, eventually troubling images and memories will no longer bother you.

Q: I have several bad habits that I would be very happy to let go of. But how? I am not a meditator.

A: If you start off not being what you need to be, where can you go? However, we can use another vocabulary.

Habits are very, very quick to engage and go into operation. For instance, if you were a caustic, sarcastic person—or, to be more precise, if you displayed that kind of behavior—even if you saw the problems this caused in your relationships, trying to control this behavior would still be very hard. It's the same with smoking. The cigarette appears magically in your mouth, lit, and there you are blowing smoke out of your nose. Fait accompli. And just yesterday you decided to quit.

Because habits engage so quickly, you must make the mind alert and even quicker. You can do this with exercises that undercut physical habit patterns and, eventually, mental ones. Without strengthening and speeding up the mind, the habits will always be a step ahead of you.

Q: I have taken vows and made promises to myself many times. Every New Year's Day I proclaim that I am finished with cigarettes and alcohol. Six to eight weeks later, these vows disintegrate and I am left back where I started—except that I've humiliated myself again. Why do I keep blowing it?

A: The person who made the promise isn't the same one who breaks it. Wisdom, which is a positive energy, generated the vow; ignorance, a negative energy, generated the breach.

Everyone has both these energies, the evolutionary and the destructive. By cultivating wisdom through meditation, a shift toward a vigilant awareness occurs and ignorance is no longer able to fool us quite so easily. Then the wisdom energy that initiates skillful action can sustain whatever we undertake. You are then able to sustain your vows because wisdom acts as a security system, protecting you.

When we decide to change our behavior, it is useful if we take a little time to perform a ritual to underscore the commitment to change. To a cynic, any ritual looks silly and feels embarrassing. But for someone who knows how to use them, rituals mark a moment in time with a powerful gesture. The moment they mark is *now,* for change can only occur in the present moment. We add weight to our intention when we include spiritual elements in the ritual. It becomes a spiritualized ritual, a sacred ritual.

I take candles, incense, and flowers to the little altar in my room. I place things that have meaning and significance in my life on this altar: photos of saints, family members, good friends, beings who have left this world, beings who have just recently arrived, and a photo of myself as a child. In performing a ritual, we dedicate the goodness that will arise from our vow to all the beings who we have brought to our consciousness, and then to all beings in the world, whether living or dead.

When we take a vow, we should vow for life. We can say we vow for life since this present moment marks a transition toward something better. Right in the very moment we vow to behave differently, we weaken a link in the chain of habits that binds us to the wheel of becoming, and we move a step closer toward our freedom.

Q: Since I began watching my mind, I have noticed that it is full of wicked thoughts. They come and go all through the day and even in my dream life. Sometimes I find a perverted interest in them and watch them for quite a while, like movies. I don't do this with all the images that occur, but the ones I do watch often make me shudder. They come out of nowhere and I can't stop them.

A: Since you are already a meditator, I will answer this in a way so you can pursue this matter in your own practice. First, who said these thoughts were wicked? Check into that. Secondly, who judges your thoughts? Thirdly, who observes the movies? As you contemplate these questions, you might also ask yourself, "What do these thoughts have to do with my life?"

One of the insights that will come to you in this contemplation is that good thoughts also arise out of nowhere. The thoughts you like, the thoughts you dislike, and the thoughts you are indifferent toward mostly come and go on their own. This is an extraordinary insight for Westerners, because it is so different from our assumed understanding of the mind. Growing up in a matrix of Judeo-Christian thought, we are inclined to think in terms of good and evil, angelic and satanic. So we categorize certain kinds of thoughts as good and certain ones as evil.

In terms of meditation, this causes unnecessary suffering. The thoughts you speak of in themselves are neither good nor bad. They come from nowhere and return to nowhere. They belong only to nature. If you want to be free from fear, guilt, and shame, you need to abandon the judging of thoughts and establish a new, more skillful attitude with the help of proper meditation practice.

People become anxious about the images and moods that come up in their practice. A skillful meditator recognizes these as gestalts, patterns of behavior that have no power to injure us.

They are just functions of the process of thought. Thoughts intimidate us because we have not yet understood their nature—that they belong to no one. When we understand that what we understand is not me or mine, there is freedom.

Q: I'm beginning to be more painfully aware of how much conflict, confusion, and suffering is going on in my mind. Where is the end to this situation?

A: The end comes when you complete the job of purifying your mind. The conditions that generated the state of your mind as you now observe it have already occurred and produced their effects. You can't stop what is already done. But you can stop adding to the situation by letting go of thoughts as soon as they are prompted by the sense organs or memory, letting them pass on by. By not compounding the situation, the habit of letting things stick to your mind and bother you will gradually change. In this new mental climate, the old memories, attitudes, opinions, and emotional biases will fade away quite naturally.

However, even after these bothersome elements fade away, there still lurks the last remaining pollutant that the magic whitener of letting go can't quite eliminate. For that to go too, we have to allow the bottom to fall out of our hopes, plans, and relationship to a sense of self. The world of delusion along with the conflict it creates collapses, and the last remnants of suffering collapse with it. Then there is only knowing in the pure sense.

If you don't watch your mind, who will? If the mind is left on its own without an observer, what does it do? And when there is an observer, what does the mind do?

The observer is on top of every situation: memory, fantasy, plans, revenge, compassion, doubts. It is the nature of the mind to run about searching for things to get involved with. The observer sees all this.

Learn to observe the observer. Bring it into your awareness and teach it to let go of everything. Letting go is Buddha-nature. The Buddha-mind becomes thoroughly bored and disgusted with the mind's endless proliferation of thoughts and involvement with nothing of substance—and lets go.

CHAPTER SEVEN

Being in the Present

Q: I can't figure out the concept of time at all. I see that when I think back on something, that memory is a moment in time. Then I remember the present and—zip! it's another moment in time. These flashbacks into the past and "blink-backs" into the present switch back and forth, like a slide show presentation. I don't have a feeling for the difference. Where can we stand and actually observe the passage of time?

A: A good glimpse into the world of time requires the perspective of the present moment, for in the present moment we can see that time is a concept created by the mind, that it is merely a belief. If we are not grounded in the present, we get absorbed in time-bound memories and are drowned in time. We see the world as made up of discrete experiences rather than as a continuously moving flow.

If you look carefully, you'll see that memories are not fixed things, like slides, but are more like mini-movies. You said that you could jump from remembering the past to remembering the present. If you are only remembering the present, it is as if you are living in the past. If this makes the present a sort of virtual reality, then for myself I have to say I prefer the old-fashioned, natural, handwritten version.

You don't need to remember the present; you need to *be* the present. The present is the truth, for nothing happens in the present and everything happens in the present.

Q: I believe meditators can train themselves to be able to visit the future or go back in time to visit the historical past. Is this a skill I can learn quickly?

A. This is what you already do most of the time! You visit the past when you "click" on memory. You are instantly propelled into the event you are recalling, and then you add all kinds of emotional components to that memory byte. Again, the past is regurgitated as a projection into the future. This is not much different from memory of the past, except that the future is born out of a mind bent on hopes, plans, or fantasies. This is the "forward" mode, and we are off and running with it.

Neither of these time travel experiences lands you in reality. The past and future threaten to overwhelm the present, since our habits shift us in and out of these dream states, "forward" and "reverse."

Have you ever wondered where you would be without a

past or future? Or who you would be? You would be everywhere. You would be who you are.

Don't go farther astray from reality. Train yourself to bring the mind to the here and now, and be awake.

The future, built out of the past, is the great distracter. We want the future to be rosy, all fun and happiness. But all our hopes and dreams sabotage the possibility of a happy future simply because they make us miss the present.

I find this even after all these years of spiritual training. Sometimes when I am walking alone down a country road, free of responsibilities and worldly dealings, my old urban habits nevertheless induce the mind to think and worry about how much farther I need to go before I arrive where I'm going. The big joke is that this way of thinking emerges even though I can arrive almost anywhere, anytime. I can set up my umbrella just about anywhere—the next village, the village after that, or just here off the road where there is water and a flat bit of land. The notion of time and space still dogs my footsteps.

As I approach a village, I'll see children carrying their school books. They walk past me with a lightness born of being present—not stuck in the molasses of time-space reality. "How far" and "when" don't clog their minds.

Those of us who have lived lives determined by the clock and almost entirely by the rational mode of mind feel threatened by a lack of precise information and are tormented by memories of past mistakes. All this weighs on us more heavily than our backpacks.

Many people embrace the idea of time in order to plan for the future and make it secure. To some extent this is useful and intelligent, but the reality is that the future cannot be made secure. This should be too obvious to have to say, since our very lives are not even guaranteed into the next hour.

One of the fruits of wisdom is outgrowing the need for a future, secure or insecure. With wisdom comes an understanding of time. From the standpoint of wisdom, time is no longer the sacred construct that modern people believe it to be. The support for the reality of time is withdrawn, and time just dangles. We are free of it.

CHAPTER EIGHT

The Art of Meditation

Q: I don't know much about meditation. I've tried it a few times but I'm not sure I went about it the right way. Is there something I have to do after I cross my legs, close my eyes, and sit still?

A: Yes, there is an art to meditation. Crossing your legs and closing your eyes is just the initial step, a signal to the one inside that you are setting about developing an understanding and a proficiency in this art.

Meditation concerns the way one relates to the inner world. There are factors in the mind that need to be balanced. Therefore, you have to be exceedingly alert and determined. There are all kinds of ways to make mistakes in meditation. I reckon I've made them all.

The skillful meditator has to keep on correcting, realigning, and staying alert. When the yogi gets this right, I call it "sitting in the Buddha." In the Buddha is contained the Dharma—

enlightened, natural wisdom. Most of us can get it right some of the time. However, sitting in the Buddha is a dynamic condition. We practice extending and sustaining it through mindfulness and observation.

Almost everyone can meditate. It is important to understand right from the beginning where you are going with your meditation, why you are going there, and how to go about the journey properly. If you just force yourself to sit still with your eyes closed and legs crossed without a goal or a vision, you will soon abandon this exercise for something more interesting and less painful.

Q: What meditation technique can you recommend for me? May I ask which ones you have had extensive experience with?

A: There is a whole spectrum of techniques that have been used by sages since ancient times. It is impossible for anyone to be familiar with all of them. Ancient Eastern texts and commentaries list dozens of these techniques and describe skillful ways to develop them. Some are more general, while others are appropriate for particular personality types or stages of spiritual development. Some address the more destructive energies, like lust and greed. One of the contemporary classics on meditation is by Ajahn Buddhadasa Bhikkhu. The technique he masterfully describes—focusing on the breath at various levels of refined awareness—has been a useful mode of practice for many meditators. You should at least become familiar with this way of practice.

I have had considerable experience with five or six techniques. Each one turns the mind toward an object on which we can fix our attention. The technique is then developed and cultivated through patient practice. The techniques I have incorporated in my practice use as the object of awareness the movement of the body, the fluctuations in the mind between the poles of fear and desire, the inner sound current that seems to be constantly ringing in our consciousness, the spaces between the mental and physical phenomena where conceptualization has no place to attach, the bones supporting the body which we term collectively the skeleton, and death as the end of a beginning and the beginning of an ending. Any one of these practices can lead you toward the wisdom you need to perfect your life and gain the freedom you hunger for.

I can alert you to particular things that come up in practice so that you don't repeat the mistakes I made. Undoubtedly, though, you will go ahead and make your own mistakes—and of course you will learn more from these than from your smooth-flowing experiences.

You will find comprehensive overviews of meditation in many meditation manuals available in bookstores, and these should address most of your concerns. One facet of meditation you are not likely to come upon as you review those manuals, however, is the importance of beginning your practice with the right view and the right attitude. Maintaining these is important for your efforts to bear appropriate fruits. This is no easy matter, for it means that you endeavor to set yourself where you can see the limitations of any technique and its relationship to its goal. The end will only manifest itself fully when both technique and meditator slip away and the deeper dimensions of awareness shine through. A raft is a tool for crossing a river. Reaching the other riverbank, the wise will set the raft aside and continue on their way, burdened by nothing. In the same way, the technique takes us where we want to go, and then we leave it behind.

Because the nature of true meditation practice is close to a catch-22 situation, novice meditators need careful and thorough orientation to their practice. If you are not grounded in your practice closely enough to the teachings of the Buddha and his wise disciples, you may simply head off in any interesting direction. You might end up with supernatural powers that would enable you to fly, levitate, see the past, or know the minds of others. You would become a fascinating, powerful person capable of extraordinary feats, but you would have missed the top prize, the pot of gold, by not going all the way to the end of the rainbow.

Q: Why do all the meditation books require that we sit in a cross-legged position? I can't sit that way for more than three minutes!

A: These days most meditation books suggest other options as well, such as sitting on a straight-backed chair. The posture of the body is not primary. It is the posture of the mind that needs to be straight, alert, and receptive.

Hold the resolve that you are seeking truth in order to live at peace in this world. If you come to your sitting place with the intention of learning, with the intention of realizing the truth, your mind will be occupied with this intent. Then the discomfort of your body is likely to shift quickly, and you won't be so distracted by pain. Even sitting in a comfortable chair becomes unbearable after a few hours.

Q: What can I expect to gain from meditation?

A: From the position of inquiry that comes from effective meditation we can see clearly how fear permeates our lives and how desire drives us crazy. You have probably noticed already that much of our day is spent repeating familiar patterns and following basic instincts. Karma, memory, fear, and desire for pleasure—these form the circle that pretty much circumscribes our lives. We can also talk about eating and procreation, but these activities are common to the animals as well. We humans are more complex, more easily hurt, and suffer in many more ways than they. We are subject to a kaleidoscope of psychological and emotional states, and yet are often ignorant of how to respond to them. Thus we suffer tremendously. Blind to the habitual, mechanical nature of our responses to the things of this world, we don't know just how confined we are until we practice opening the mind.

With mature meditation practice comes an inner appreciation of the ability of the mind to distance itself from the world in virtually all aspects.

Skillful meditation is practice in letting go. In letting go of the things we customarily cling to, we find a freedom we only tasted as children, or stepped into by sheer accident as a teenager walking along an isolated beach, or got a glimpse of while hiking alone in a national park. The miracle that can happen to us, the miracle awaiting us, is recognizing the workings of the prison that binds our life, and then walking the path out of this prison and into freedom. Freedom is the essence of the spiritual quest. For one who practices diligently, more and more openings appear through which freedom can be known, until finally all that unfolds in one's life is timeless freedom. We realize this as the ultimate happiness—peace, enlightenment.

Q: When I have free time, I start thinking about going to my sitting corner to meditate. But once this idea has come to my mind, I feel tired. This often happens at night, after a day at the office. Am I tired or lazy?

A: You have to sort out this kind of problem for yourself. Certainly, it is important to be able to recognize the difference between tiredness and laziness so you can act accordingly.

Try to push through the energy lag, and see what comes of your effort. You will know if you are really tired, in which case you should take a short rest. The main thing is not to brood over this. In fact, not thinking about things beyond a quick, careful observation of them is one of the skills we learn through meditation practice.

Q: Why do I get a headache when I meditate?

A: Do you ever get headaches when you don't meditate?

Q: . . . uh, yes.

A: There it is. You get headaches because you have a head.

Q: I am becoming intrigued with the practice of *vipassana* (insight meditation). Can you give me some guidance?

A: Maintain an attitude of humility as you investigate the mind. That is, try to see things as an intelligent, sensitive child would. What you need to understand deeply is obscured by your self-conceit and ignorance. Don't become too fascinated with what you find, especially with thoughts. It is all right to be fascinated to the point of awe at the process of thoughts unfolding in the mind. This is skillful. But don't become fascinated with thoughts in a way that you get stuck in them. Learn to be free enough to be able to let go of everything.

Your duty as a meditator is to simply get out of the way and let everything run down. Learn to discern the nature of wisdom so that you can cultivate it with confidence. Wisdom eradicates ignorance. The two are incompatible.

Q: What is the point of trying to sit when you know your mind is going to zoom all over the place and drive you crazy?

A: Good question. And an inevitable one. First, recognize that this crazy mind is sitting harmlessly on a cushion not bothering anyone—except you. Sitting quietly, you're not going to be colliding into other people's minds, which are also running wild and unharnessed. Take refuge in the wisdom of moving yourself out of danger.

While you are sitting with this crazy mind, you can observe it. This may feel uncomfortable, since you cannot control the mind. The mind is following its own nature—shooting out here, there, and everywhere. The mind doesn't concern itself with what kinds of mischief it gets into.

But to emphasize again, you are sitting on your cushion alone with yourself. You're not in the midst of society. This is an important distinction. Your mind will slow down and the spinning will cease, whereas the mind in the marketplace has no chance to cease spinning. It necessarily keeps bumping into things that trigger the proliferation of thoughts and create karma.

Be assured that the mind on the cushion will wind down. In a short while, say forty minutes, the spinning will be subdued. Sometime later, the chaos that comes from vagrant thoughts jumping into a hot, spinning mind will also cease. You will be sitting in the coolness of the peaceful mind.

Take refuge in knowing that sitting meditation is the best thing you can do to quiet and focus the mind. The quiet, focused mind has access to wisdom, and this wisdom will get you through every time.

There will be many times when the mind is spinning in such utter confusion that the only little bit of wisdom able to come through is the suggestion: "Go and just sit quietly."

Follow that advice. Don't try to add to it or do anything too fancy. Accept the confusion. Don't be intimidated by the thought that you are just wasting time. You're not. When that thought comes, simply reflect upon the fact that there is no time, whether you understand the reality of this statement or not.

The mind will automatically begin to settle down. When you sit, you slow down the confusion and chaos. The more often you train yourself this way, the faster the mind can respond to agitation and disturbance. If you don't apply the brakes, the mind just spins further out into more madness.

Q: Isn't the point of meditation to stop the mind? I've tried to do this, but it seems impossible.

A: We can't really stop the mind. Occasionally, it will stop on its own. What we can do while the mind is whirling in perpetual motion is recognize that this is the mind's very nature. As meditators seeking freedom, we can practice not getting stuck in anything that the mind happens to land upon.

What is meant by the phrase "stopping the mind" is precisely this ability to stop the mind short of its habit of holding and grasping. This is the mark of psychological freedom. Enlightenment is the freedom to let go of everything—immediately.

Q: Is there a reward for practicing meditation?

A: Yes, the best, the highest possible reward, the grand prize to end all prizes. Meditation, in whatever form, makes us more alert, aware, and clear—especially about oneself, whoever or whatever that is. That alertness, combined with wise contemplation, will lead to inner freedom, the ultimate prize.

We spend our days and nights focused on ourselves and our personal melodramas. This thicket of self-centeredness closes us off from the world around us, and we become the center of a small, mundane world. Sitting opens us up to the world. It provides the leverage to enter into, yet rise above the world.

There is only one world. But it appears radically different in both depth and scope through these two experiences. The one, our personal world, is conditioned by sense-perceptions, instincts, habits, time-space, and karma. The other world is free. We are free to observe, free to probe the unknown in whichever direction the way leads us. As human beings we have the opportunity to choose between these two.

Sit. Sit some more. When we begin to sit, we sit with ourselves. In the end, the universe sits in us.

CHAPTER NINE

Seeing the Whole Picture

Q: A friend who meditates tells me that none of this is real. I have tried to understand what she is saying but I don't get it. Things don't always seem real to me; but on the other hand, when I am sick or heartbroken, everything feels *too* real.

A: Perhaps your friend had a mini enlightened moment. I don't know. If we assume she is relating an understanding that comes via insight, we can only say that what she is trying to describe is indescribable. However, when the mind is focused and alert and we are observing the nature of consciousness from inside the mind, we can experience the fact that all conditions just arise and pass away in rapid continuous succession. Things are merely appearances that don't belong to anyone. The "anyone" they might belong to is a fabrication that comes into being, passes away, and comes back together in a similar form again and again.

Birth—death—birth. Disintegration—regeneration—

disintegration. In the eyes of most people, this process seems real and substantial. To those with eyes to see, it's all a movie. The difference between these two modes of seeing is profound. Those who see only the concrete, material world see only the surface. Their lives move along on the surface. They see the front of things without ever seeing the back. They live with all the problems that come from partial vision.

Those who see with penetrating eyes see the whole picture. They see the surface and they see the depths of things. They see through and around. They live both in the world and aloof from it. Their insight into the nature of the world comes from diligent spiritual practice. They are not caught in the conventions of life and are not living merely in a conceptual reality.

Q: Is there a way to stimulate profundity within the mind?

A: Profound events and moments happen on their own.

Q: If I were to look out into the world as a wise person, what would I see? *(A question from a 10-year-old child.)*

A: You would see a world full of creatures, each one of them carrying the burden of previous disharmonious and improper actions. The taint or scar left from that foolishness is called karma.

A wise person sees a world full of beings forced to carry what is hard to bear, and so compassion arises in him. The wise person then goes on to help others in the best fashion he can.

You won't be able to understand this yet—or maybe you do understand the implications of what I am saying. But no adult has ever asked me the question you just asked.

Q: I have read a lot about Zen Buddhism and am impressed with the number of koans that there are. But is there one koan that is the most important?

A: The Buddha solved the great koan embedded in this universe. All Buddhas solve the same koan and thereby set the wheel of Dharma rolling. What is the great koan? All that arises passes away.

Every school child knows this. This fact is so blatantly obvious that it is likely to be taken at face value without recognizing its transformative power. Only a budding Buddha would consider this theorem to be profound. That's the kind of intuitive wisdom and determination that makes bodhisattvas—Buddhas to be—unique.

The Buddha of this age, Siddhartha, scrutinized this koan, though to others it may have seemed a preoccupation with the prosaic. He focused his attention on it, knowing that his lack of true understanding of this principle maintained the sense of self and the whole mass of suffering that comes along with this notion.

All that arises passes away. Reflect upon this principle and observe what arises and passes away in your mind.

Q: When does the beginningless begin?

A: The beginningless begins forever!

Q: Buddhism recognizes wisdom as the objective of the religious life. Does that mean that a supercomputer can become an enlightened being?

A: Hardly. Both computers and wisdom make use of data, but that is as far as the similarity goes. From my viewpoint, a supercomputer is just an expensive toy. I am not impressed by a machine even if it can access huge amounts of information in a blink of an eye. Of what value is data?

With wisdom, however, I am very, very impressed. For after wisdom receives data, it immediately and spontaneously assesses the situation. That is, wisdom sees the way things are in the present moment deeply and comprehensively. Then it responds objectively and with *metta*, loving kindness. I would say that a Buddha represents the ultimate potentiality for integrating wisdom and loving kindness into every moment of thought. I can safely say that no one will ever develop a computer with this capacity, even with a billion years of cutting-edge technological research.

Q: I know that the truth is supposed to be incredibly simple, but if I try to act in as simple a way as possible, often I look—and feel—like a fool.

A: There is a fine line between simple as in genius and simple as in simpleton. The genius and the fool can utter the same words and make similar gestures, but in the case of the fool, the words and gestures are inconsequential and meaningless; in the case of the wise person, these same words and gestures carry authority. By authority I mean the presence of truth grounded in radiating love.

An intriguing paradox in this universe is that things that appear to be straightforward may actually have two diametrically opposing faces. When your heart is clear and full of love, you will know the simplicity of a sage. You won't have any problem discerning the difference between simplicity and Simplicity.

Q: When do we come to know the-way-things-are?

A: Only after we have come to know the way things aren't.

Watching my mind, all I see are patterns of thought, feelings, perceptions, and so on constantly arising and passing away. All of them are interrelated, for all are made out of the same mind stuff. No exemptions. This is incontrovertible evidence that the world exists as a complete whole and the things of the world exist as modifications of that. In mathematical terms, all the knowable dimensions of the world are contained in a circle, which has no beginning or end.

Even though knowing intuitively that reality is coherent, we can make a problem out of it, and then require scientists to run experiments so that the results can be monitored. Then we will have *scientific* evidence that there is a fundamental compatibility, thus proving that all things are essentially the same. But in the end, regardless of how many experiments are done, how many rivers are harnessed to fuel monitoring equipment, and how many technicians are gainfully employed, the experience of knowing is ultimately left to us, isn't it?

CHAPTER TEN

The Monastic Lifestyle

Q: You practiced for several years as a layman before becoming a monk. What do you find to be the biggest difference between the two, or the major benefit of ordination?

A: Comparing the spiritual environment in a monastic community with the spiritual environment in lay life, the most prominent difference is the degree of commitment and consistency. The *sangha*, the monastic environment, is designed to provide a spiritual edge so that those who have the courage to practice diligently can do so. The lay life requires time and energy to be spent in meeting the responsibilities of family life and the demands of a full-time job. This is the way it is for most people.

There are a few rare individuals capable of practicing diligently in the world itself. They can create their own spiritual environment. For them, the marketplace and the high-walled monastery are on an even playing field.

Q: You have been living the life of a monk for quite a while. What lead you to take the robes? Or perhaps I want to ask, what do you consider the biggest advantage of living as a monastic?

A: Before I became a monk, I found that the world would sabotage my good intentions and considerable efforts at every turn. Contemporary society is ever so willing to bend to accommodate our most frivolous desires. So whenever I made a slip, lost myself, or lost my commitment to living simply and quietly—baam! everything would collapse and I would find myself back at square one.

Monastic life is much more contained, much more supportive of my commitment to simplicity, quietude, and contemplation.

Q: When I visited your monastery, I spoke with one monk there for about half an hour. After a few minutes, I got the distinct impression that the monk's mind was in worse shape than mine. It is possible that meditation practice could take someone farther out of a meditative frame of mind?

A: You should have met that monk before! In the monasteries where I have lived, I have always seen people improving.

Some arrive in dreadful shape but somehow have both the wisdom and the merit to enter into a commitment to meditate.

Monasteries are like hospitals. Some of us are still in the intensive care unit. Some are relatively healed and are helping others. Some will leave and practice in the world. It is not easy to live this life fully. The few who can do it will remain, maintain their commitment, and carry the tradition forward. The great legacy they will leave is the continuation of the tradition.

Don't bother to judge others. Those you see practicing in monasteries are doing the best they can. Some are walking up a very steep incline. If you appear to be healthier than someone else, just see that as appearance and drop it. Watch the mind continuously, and use your experiences to awaken to the-way-things-are. Practice is the determination to observe and investigate the mind always.

Q: I have long thought about staying in a Buddhist monastery for the six months of vacation time that I have accumulated. But I know that people in the monasteries of your tradition eat only food begged as alms and eat only once a day, in the morning. The wake-up bell is rung at 3:00 A.M., and every day there are chores that everybody shares. All this sounds too extreme for me. Can you suggest a monastic community that isn't so tough?

A: In Asia there are all kinds of monastic communities that provide the kind of opportunity you are looking for. But you will find some aspects in each of them that will not suit you. I don't know much about monasteries other than the ones I have lived in except by hearsay, so I can't help you much there.

Keep in mind as you are considering these places that things are relative. If you had never seen a redwood tree, you would think that a twenty-foot fir is very tall and beautiful. If all you know is three meals a day, eight hours of sleep, one hour of news, thirty minutes of balancing your checkbook, doing laundry every second day, one and a half hours of daily commuting, and fifteen minutes working the daily crossword puzzle, then naturally the monastic schedule is going to appear overwhelming. And after the initial feeling of awe disappears, you may feel aversion, or you may feel indignant that it isn't more to your liking. We all have gone through that one.

Once you get into the rhythm of a monastic lifestyle, the order of things just becomes ordinary. Not eating three times a day, not following the news, not balancing checkbooks, not scouring the daily paper for clever cartoons, not clipping discount coupons, not adding up air miles, and not fiddling with leaky faucets becomes just another way of life, one that frees up a lot of time and space. Then you will have the chance to understand a great deal more about yourself than you do now.

The community activities such as doing chores together, chanting together in the early morning, and walking for alms help to keep everyone going in the same direction. They promote harmony in the community and help the individual to develop and sustain a valuable meditation practice.

Q: Do you find the diet and way of eating in your monastery—with the various foods gathered from begging all mixed together—to be helpful spiritually, or is it just a convenient way to deal with getting food into the body?

A: At the very least, I regard monastic life as a key to opening doors and windows that are ordinarily shut. With my ordination I resolved to eat a single meal a day in the morning, as dictated by our tradition. I soon began to notice many unusual things about eating that had otherwise escaped my attention.

One very interesting quirk was that I would feel more hunger *after* eating than before. That was strange. Obviously, there was a hunger within me that was not satiated by food. I investigated that for a long time. As I worked with it around my meal, I was able to sort out all kinds of stuff and to disentangle a lifetime of distorted and conflicting messages regarding food for the body and food for the heart. I could then use that understanding to see deeply into my mind where the core ignorance lives and binds me to the wheel of becoming. This is the secret hideout from where foolishness, greed, and clinging contaminate our life. This process and many other experiences and insights have lightened my life and widened my range of choices.

With food, I now find that I can take it or leave it and am just as happy with one kind of food as I am with another. I have the freedom to eat what is available and be content with it. This is the priority before any other consideration—even whether the food is vegetarian or not. So, for me, eating rather quickly what is offered once a day, in silence and with appreciation, is spiritually productive as well as efficient.

Q: Why are monks not allowed to watch TV?

A: To avoid distraction. The commitment to take ordination is a determined effort to turn away from petty diversions such as hobbies, reading pulp fiction, and indulging in sports and games. These only serve to take the mind away from what is really worthwhile. Taking ordination is a commitment to die to the superfluous.

Television, video games, shopping, and the like hardly give the mind a chance to become grounded. When we're watching TV, we think we are keeping up with important events of the world. But once we understand that the world operates without moral values and mostly through power and exploitation, the actual events become inconsequential—the countries change, the leaders with their distorted and selfish desires make a few plays in the world and then disappear. If we hang on to any of it, we end up fretting over it, for most new events stir up a lot of anxiety. We become embroiled in the news at our own peril. For people who can see through this, there are other, more important things to occupy the mind with.

Q: There is a movement in the United States to liberalize the rules for monks so they can adjust to the times and fit into the culture more smoothly. What do you think about this ?

A: I think that if the distinction between monks and lay-persons becomes blurred, everyone will be the worse for it. The monk will have compromised his integrity in order to meet other people's concerns, and the laity will lose much more than they realize. The monastic community carries the lineage of the *dharma vinaya,* the Buddhist teachings as encompassed in the monastic vows, in its entirety. The only way this tradition can be handed down through time in its pure state is by people actually living it.

The lifestyle of the *bhikkhu* has been designed to help individuals turn away from the world and look into the truth of things. They are able to know and pass on aspects of the teaching that can only be realized through the deep understanding that comes from full-time inquiry. This wisdom is invaluable, the most precious thing in the world.

Q: There is a general belief that most monks and nuns take ordination because they are heartbroken. Was this true for you?

A: If people believe that, then nothing or no one can change their minds. However, in the monasteries, I have rarely met anyone romantically brokenhearted. To take on this level of commitment to spiritual life requires more motivation than that.

In a sense, though, I could say that I took ordination because I was heartbroken—heartbroken because the world is as it is. Suffering, conflict, poverty, exploitation, and injustice are rampant, and little is done to address these urgent problems. Unlike some other Western monks whom I know, I wasn't depressed, suppressed, or incapable of living an ordinary life. I simply opted for a better way to live. I was keenly aware of all the pain in the world as you and I know it. I became thoroughly disenchanted and bored with what the world had to offer. The reality of our human situation broke my heart. I am striving toward the way beyond.

Q: What do the monks do about the hoards of mosquitoes that live in the forests and caves where the monks reside?

A: We don't do anything.

Many years ago, I caught a mosquito in a large-mouthed bottle. It had been buzzing around my cave for hours. When I finally trapped it in the bottle, I tried to reprogram it through telepathic suggestion into believing that it was a butterfly and should behave like one. Two days later I released it inside my mosquito net. It circled around me a few times and helped itself to another bite of my arm.

This confirmed for me that mosquitoes know just one way of behavior—and also confirmed my lack of telepathic prowess! The mosquitoes are acting the way they should. It is we humans who see a problem where there is none. It is we who must change. This is part of the Buddhist practice of letting go. Learning to coexist with everything is part of becoming a mature person.

PART THREE

Bringing the Forest Home

Work out your own salvation with diligence.

—The Buddha's last words

P erhaps the most traveled path in our world today is the information super-highway. This cyber-infrastructure has penetrated even
the most remote villages, where people still use beasts of burden as their
transportation. Truly, we are well on our way to making a great array of
information available at the fingertips of everyone. Yet this proliferation of knowledge has not brought us any closer to truth. In fact, the
more we listen to the many false prophets around us, the less we hear
the voice of truth within us.

In the Buddha's last words to his loyal disciple Ananda, he encouraged all those who had spent their lives listening to him to apply
the Dharma in their lives. Therein, he said, lies our salvation. For it is
only by taking up the path that we move closer to enlightenment. And
it is only in the act of doing good that goodness becomes a reality for us.

CHAPTER ONE

Living the Answers

Q: Usually I come home from work in a state of frenzy after a one-hour commute through heavy traffic. I need to find some peace right away. How can I go about it?

A: Demanding peace as a quick fix every time your mind becomes crazy will inevitably bring you disappointment. This is known as *tanha,* or craving. This sort of craving, the Buddha said, leads straight to suffering because we cannot really control the mind according to our wishes.

What will bring tranquillity to your mind is acceptance of what is—the willingness to be with whatever arises. Whatever is happening, be it frenzy or delight, you learn to accept. Note the characteristics of your mind's condition. In particular, note its pattern of arising and passing away. Everything that arises in your mind passes away; these conditions are merely visitors.

Occasionally your concentration will develop into a

peaceful state of mind. This is probably what you want to happen "right away." Isn't this like what electronics companies advertise as "entertainment on demand?" Demanding a certain state of mind sabotages the opportunity for that very thing to happen.

Understanding what factors cause us to fall so far out of balance is important. What drives us crazy? Identify the causal connections so you can solve the problem at its source. You will see that you get into a state of frenzy from running against the world so hard. The wise shift their approach to the world to a way that takes them *above* the world.

Q: I take one day a week out of my hectic life and practice meditation from 6:00 A.M. to 8:00 P.M. For the first hours my mind is often restless and busy-minded. Then a transition takes place and things smooth out. By the evening I am much more clear and alert—usually. However, sometimes the restlessness and busy-mindedness carry on the whole day. When this happens, is there something I can do to get a few minutes of that peace of mind that I long for?

A: Don't long for anything. Just keep investigating the states of your mind. As an impartial, open-minded observer, don't judge any mind state as better than another. This attitude will promote the peace you are seeking.

When we are looking for something or other, we set ourselves up for the disappointment that comes with not getting what we want. Don't set yourself up for suffering by coming into your practice with expectations.

Sometimes the mind is wild and nutty, sometimes serene and peaceful. Wisdom is the attitude of accepting things as they are. Wisdom recognizes that all conditions are changing, are apt to be unsatisfactory, and don't belong to the meditator.

Spending one day a week in practice alone or with spiritual friends is a praiseworthy way to make good use of free time. A feeling of inner development will arise and begin to overlap both ends of your meditation day. That is, before your day of practice, the mind will begin to prepare and purify itself in readiness; afterwards, you will find your Dharma practice carrying over into the workplace. This will encourage you to further strengthen your commitment to your practice.

As you experience these direct benefits, you will begin to make a habit of sitting every day, even if only for five minutes before going to work. As your practice evolves, your meditation day will expand into meditation days, for you will discover how to meditate in the midst of the tensions at work.

What if everyone followed this? What a different world we would soon create.

Q: I am very interested in committing a long period of time to intensive meditation practice. However, I have a high-paying and interesting job aboard an Alaskan cargo ship. If I quit my job in order to practice intensively, they won't take me back because a lot of people want my job. And if I find that I have had enough meditation practice or that it's not for me, I will be without a job and with nothing but my savings to support me. How can I deal with this conflict? I feel trapped in this situation.

A: Don't make a problem out of it. All you need to do is bring more and more awareness into your life on the ship. As you increase your mindfulness, you will gain spiritual insights that will shape the course of your life. This is a lot easier than you think. Right now you have created an either/or dilemma, which only causes suffering and conflict—although it also gives you a great opportunity to examine doubt, indecision, confusion, and fear. You are suffering solely because of your fabricated misperceptions. Examine these. The future will unfold itself.

Q: I can't seem to find the right place to keep my meditation practice going. There are too many interruptions at home and at the meditation center nearby. I would like to attend retreats but cannot afford to be away for long periods from work. Where can I go?

A: Sometimes the idea comes to leave everything behind and go into a forest to practice. The thought that there are too many disturbances and that you need to be in a different, more suitable environment is a trick of the mind that keeps the meditator in doubt and discontentment. It can be disempowering. Disturbances come from our own heart. Don't be so easily deceived into thinking that where you are is inappropriate or unsuitable. On the other hand, this is not to say that moving to other places is never useful. It all depends.

An important aspect of proper meditation practice is quelling the perception that things we don't like are disturbances. Make sure you are able to discriminate between factors that make for an unsuitable formal meditation environment and factors that arise already saturated with aversion.

Most of the forest monks I associate with here in Asia say no place is remote enough to be out of the range of motorcycles and boom-boxes.

Q: I know I could be doing more in my life spiritually and feel guilty that I am not. It's a dilemma for me.

A: The fact is that you are already doing as much as you are capable of doing well. There is always the possibility of doing more, and that possibility can become tied up with guilt and doubt. Your life is quite busy with responsibilities to your children and husband. If you undertook to do more practice, you would be taking quality time from your existing commitments.

Many of us identify with high-minded ideals about how the world should be or how we should be, and then take them on as our social or spiritual conscience. A voice inside harasses us to do more, to be better, to not be lazy, and the rest, making for a nasty bundle of contrived guilt. This guilt can dishearten us and weaken our resolve to progress in life.

What you should do is what you are obliged to do, but in a better way. Work constantly at improving your relationships with

other people and with the things in your life. If you practice re-
straining your superficial desires and try to do the best you can
under all conditions, your life is bound to progress. Work from
where you are, from your present level of awareness. Later, new
interests will emerge, and you will be prepared to live them
through. They too will pass away, and the next things will emerge.
And so it goes.

Q: I am a judge in a municipal court. Last week I had to
sentence a good man who made only one bad mistake to life in
prison. This is the first time I have had to hand down such a
severe penalty. The homicide resulted from a series of unfortunate misunderstandings. Frankly, I have been agonizing over this
decision since the pretrial hearing.

A: The world and the Dharma are at odds, you see. The
world flows in a different direction than the principles of compassion that you cherish in your heart. The world is mostly interested in survival at any cost. There is no end to the injustices that
occur every day, no end to the situations that don't accord with
loving kindness.

You have studied Buddhist principles and learned that everyone has to face the karmic consequences of the actions they
do with intention. We know that it would be a far better solution
for criminals to spend the rest of their lives rectifying their mistakes by serving others than for them to be locked up behind
bars. But no one dares to look at this situation with wisdom. If

criminals were helped to see the workings of their karma and were given a chance to develop their minds and learn to control their behavior, when they eventually died, they would do so in peace, without anger and bitterness. It is the force of these unskillful feelings that sets up their future births as beings who are even more destructive than before. Casting human beings into high-tech dungeons is a short-sighted and compassionless approach to crime.

What I am saying is right for an ideal world. You, as an appointed judge, however, have a certain duty in the conventional world. You must therefore carry out the will of the state as required. You must honor your duty. At the same time, by remaining faithful to your spiritual path of meditation and developing wisdom, you will also preserve your innate compassion. In this way, you will find many opportunities to help people during your years of service to the state.

Q: I would like to meditate regularly, but I love music. I don't think they go together—or do they? What about musical meditation tapes? Would they be acceptable?

A: You're right, they don't usually go together. In most cases, music doesn't help create a suitable environment for meditation. Music distracts the mind, drawing it to itself and engaging it there.

Music produced for meditation is designed to soothe the mind. This, too, engages and absorbs one's consciousness and disables the mind from either investigating or releasing the things it clings to. Meditation music is just music for relaxing; it produces a kind of sleep. This may be useful when the mind is hyperactive or tumbling about in anxiety. But it doesn't encourage meditation in the true sense: as a skillful means for waking up and seeing the truth of things.

If you pay attention to your emotional cycles, you will notice that music often leads to depression. First we get excited by the music we love. We listen to it with friends and that deepens the experience. We think about it often and search it out to hear it again. The search leads to frustration and disappointment because later experiences can't replicate the original. Our memory deceives us. The same sounds no longer enchant us, for the music has become familiar. Having been over-stimulated, we search for sensual experiences that make us feel high again. When we can't find them, or when they don't carry the same impact for us, the mind sinks into depression. This common cycle, which is hidden behind the search for more and more pleasure, is rarely recognized.

This problem may arise with regard to craving music. However, if you can either take music or leave it, you are following the middle way, and music won't be a problem for you. You can find the middle way by observing the mind just as it is. Observing it as it is, we don't want to add anything extra. There is usually enough going on in the mind already! As we become more proficient in observing, we come to understand the nature of happiness and the way to realize peace. All the sages have pointed out the way to the empty mind, the mind that doesn't cling to anything whatsoever, which is what brings real happiness and peace. This everyone must see and learn for themselves.

If you would like to experiment with a mind that isn't passionately involved with or clinging to anything, you are invited to practice meditation. Then compare the mind that is absorbed in music with the mind that is coolly dispassionate and decide which you like better.

Q: You have been talking with us for almost two hours now. You keep emphasizing "be present in the now," "do your work in a cool and present manner," "be patient," "be centered," and the like. This all sounds well and good. But if I worked only when I was centered and cool, I wouldn't been able to get much done. I see this kind of advice as disempowering for those of us who have to work in the outside world. Maybe monks can do everything in a cool and collected manner, but some of us have responsibilities to look after.

A: I hear what you are saying. You are not seeing how doing things in a proper way is critical to the kinds of results you get from your efforts. This is a subtle point, yet essential if you want to find genuine satisfaction in your work.

It's not the size or extent of one's responsibilities that is the issue, but the way one goes about one's duties. Regardless of whether someone is contracted to oversee the United Nations or has just promised to water a friend's plants, how you go about your work will determine the results.

Q: Are you saying that things will go better if I do less but do it in a cool manner?

A: That's what I'm saying. You think that this will cost you customers and money. Yes, it's possible, but not necessarily so. One thing proper meditation teaches you through inner experience is the value of peace. If you do your duties with a cool, peaceful heart, that peace will deepen. And from that place of peace you will know what needs to be done as you go about your job.

If your emphasis is on speed, efficiency, and productivity, the result will be confusion, regardless of whether you succeed in getting the results you want or not. In fact, if you do succeed and win the prizes, you won't know what to do there at the top of the heap. Your mind will be spinning so rapidly that you won't have the balance and sensitivity to appreciate your situation fully. You won't endeavor to live in moderation and contentment, but rather will be caught up in discontent. In the midst of that confusion will arise more confusion. This is the endless cycling in *samsara* that the Buddha talked about.

Q: What do you mean when you warn us about overinvolvement in the world?

A: The world I am talking about is the one that engages our habits, instincts, fears, hopes, and all the rest that ensnare human beings. This world is constantly poised to foil our attempts to be free in the moment.

Q: If I don't desire things, nothing will happen in my life.

A: On the contrary. If you free yourself from compulsive desires for all manner of unskillful and unnecessary things, the space that is left will be filled by contentment. Contentment is a subtle and profound energy. You might think nothing will happen in your life without desire catapulting you onward. In reality, then everything good has room to happen. The contented heart is able to manifest all kinds of amazing things. It isn't limited to the nagging wants associated with who you think you are. Let contentment and silence happen in your life. Loosen your grip on the few things you crave and discover that the whole world is waiting for you.

Q: I am often quite ill. How in the world can I practice when I don't feel well?

A: Your practice is looking you right in the face, so to speak. Make use of the limitations and the focus that come with chronic illness as your practice. Is there aversion? What do you want to escape from? What do you want to replace it with? Can you fix things so they stay in place permanently? Who is it who wants things to be other than what they are? Is there value to that strategy? Here is your practice.

Q: Can you recommend a strategy for making good use of my time while waiting in long lines? It's especially difficult to be patient and accepting when I'm rushing to an important meeting and have to stand in line for a taxi.

A: Patience is a great virtue. It's wise to make use of the opportunities that present themselves every day to develop this virtue. In these kinds of situations I do two things: First, I think how fortunate I am that the line is not four times as long and that this isn't the Indian Immigration Office in Calcutta. Secondly, I increase my effort to focus on the meditation object that I work with. Every moment that my mind is with my meditation object, I know that I am doing the very best thing I can do in that moment. In fact, this line is here for my benefit. And then the queue just moves along, I get where I need to be, and everything is fine. I do not buy into exasperation or indignation. Things are as they are.

When the heart is cool, everything works out and time loses its power to make us restless and irritated.

Q: Should I endure a very difficult situation or move on to a new one?

A: Spiritual teachers throughout the ages have advised their students to endure the difficult and to live in an environment suitable for spiritual growth. These two don't necessarily fit together, do they? In fact, they may be contrary to each other.

Both suggestions are right, but at any given moment only one may be true for you. This ambiguity is because truth is beyond right and wrong. Truth isn't determined by time, and thus isn't about consistency either. It manifests differently according to circumstance. Being trans-rational, truth speaks as an inner guidance beyond the rational mind. It is this voice that is trustworthy and takes us beyond our dilemmas.

It is worth emphasizing that patient endurance is a great attribute. For instance, some cold, wintry night when the heater has broken down and the neighbor's dog is barking endlessly and you are suffering from a blistering headache after a particularly crazy day at work, can you still be calm and tranquil? Suppose the world heaps more on you: a screaming baby, and maybe an allergy that itches like hell. And on top of all this, the next day is your annual evaluation day at work, and you need to be clear-headed and alert. Can you maintain equanimity and be at ease in the midst of all this? If you can, you have tremendous power.

Things happen, but they don't happen to you. Practicing patience and endurance, you know that all these minor catastrophes, like every unpleasant condition that has ever occurred, will give way and change. This is a wise perspective to maintain in a world of uncertainty.

Chapter Two

Skillful Relationships

Q: What is the nature of true love and how does it arise?

A: True love arises in the midst of purity and goodness. This is the way we talk about it in monastic circles. We know from our own insight that the pure mind is capable of acceptance without conditions. Really, the trick is to provide space for love to arise.

The nature of love is giving. It comes from compassion and an understanding of the-way-things-are.

Q: The poet Rilke said, "It is a great undertaking just to love one person." Is this enough for one lifetime?

A: You have to decide that for yourself. But to learn to love just one person properly and appropriately is to learn to love everyone and everything. It is no insignificant undertaking. Is there anything else worth pursuing?

To love anyone or anything, there must be total, unconditional acceptance. This is the first step. And, magically, it is the last step as well.

Q: When I think about getting married, it seems like a good idea. Then I think about not getting married, and that seems like a good idea too. Can you resolve this dilemma for me?

A: In this instance I will defer to the wisdom of Daniel, a student of mine: "Whatever you do, you'll regret it!"

Most of us know from experience the difficulties of making male/female relationships work. (This is not to imply that homosexual relationships are easier or better.) Men and women are "wired" differently, and this makes a harmonious relationship inherently difficult.

We generally start out in the wrong lane. We fall into romantic love—an intrinsically problematic situation, for it is easier to fall into a foolish love than a wise one.

The nature of foolish love is to cling to what we desire. It is a false love that inevitably leads to disappointment and despair, for it reaches out and attaches. It is self-serving and shallow. This is the surest path to suffering.

To sustain a male/female relationship requires genuine love. In a relationship, genuine love is the answer to everything, whereas selfish love is the catalyst for every kind of tragic occurrence. Without genuine love, each partner can inflict all manner of abuse upon the other, for they are slaves of their desires and wants. If only one partner develops the wisdom and courage to cultivate genuine love, she can carry the relationship. In time, the other person will have the opportunity to learn by example, and if he is sensitive, will learn the way of love as well.

To love another fully is to love all and everything. To love one thing fully is to recognize the interrelationship between everything. To come to love everything, you must learn to love yourself first. Goodness will follow automatically.

Genuine love is both an offering and an acceptance. It carries no demands and makes room for things to flow. Genuine love exists *between* people—it's not fixed and attached to them. All attempts at intimacy fail unless there is a spiritually based, heartfelt commitment to establish a foundation for it in genuine love. Unless there is offering—a giving that is unhampered by wanting something reciprocal—the relationship has no feet on which to stand. Without selflessness there is only transaction.

When we cultivate love for ourselves, we recognize deeply our spiritual nature and clean out the "stuff" that obscures this reality. Our spiritual nature, which is imbued with wisdom and *metta,* is what has the capacity to love another.

Q: Can couples use meditation to support their relation-ship?

A: I would say that in this era, couples *must* use meditation to bond their relationship and to grow together in the same direc-tion.

All the defending that often arises in a relationship pushes the other away and sows the seeds for separation. When you medi-tate together, you meet on an elevated, cool common ground. This helps one to live respectfully and appropriately with the other. Then each person is willing to accept the disappointments, frus-trations, foolishness, and fear-based demands of the other.

Statistics indicate that in the present day few people can come together in an intimate relationship, commit to that rela-tionship, and then make it work. In many of the states in the United States, eight out of ten marriages and committed partner-ships fall apart within a few years.

A relationship that isn't founded properly has almost no chance of surviving the inevitable changes and challenges that arise over time. If two people come together in a primarily ro-mantic and sexual relationship, no matter how hot the romance and how passionate the sexuality, the relationship is destined to plunge into a sea of sorrow. Any relationship that functions without self-sacrifice, without nurturing, and without sufficient encouragement for both people to become free and independent has to come apart—if not physically, certainly psychologically and spiritually.

Look at a typical relationship in terms of how unenlightened minds function. Initially, the two people come together in a state of romantic enchantment and total absorption with each other. It feels great! However, soon the enchantment can no longer saturate every moment. Things change. A speck of suspicion enters their minds; something is not quite right. Right behind this speck of anxiety comes fear, and then all sorts of schemes to reconstruct things as they were, or better than they were! Now there is struggle, self-consciousness, frustration, disappointment, and all the rest.

Meanwhile, a psychological bonding between these two people has formed, and they have become attached to one another. With attachment comes fear of loss or separation. When ignorance is in charge of things, the more we fear, the more disappointment we experience, and the greater the delight, the more fiercely we cling. Delight leads us to want more, to want to continually embrace what makes us feel good. Inherent in that clinging are the seeds of suffering, which take the form of fear of change. And change inevitably occurs, which triggers stronger clinging—the struggle to maintain the status quo in a moving stream of perpetual change. The result? Broken hearts, tears, despair.

What works, then? A relationship has the best chance of lasting and bringing happiness to both partners if it is built on a foundation of selfless, nurturing service to each other. This kind of relationship can endure all manner of change, difficulty, frustration, disappointment, and the other challenges that come with living this human life together with another.

It takes a kind of intuitive genius in letting go to relate properly to another human being. When we have stepped out of the way and backed off from our personal desires, we can hear the inner need of the other, which is the need of the moment.

Q: As far back as I can remember the relationship between myself and my mother has been full of hostility, alienation, and ill-will. In therapy as a young adult, I was told by my therapist that beneath all the icy aversion, my parents really had a well-spring of love for me. I recognized that it would be natural for it to be that way.

Now another fifteen years have gone by and things are still basically the same. I can honestly say that I've done nothing to deepen the rift, and yet the situation remains the same as when I was a child. I've studied Eastern philosophies and practiced yoga and meditation for many years, so I understand something about karma and a bit about the human mind. And truly, I don't see a well-spring of love either within my mother or within myself. Given this situation, how is it possible to shift things?

A: Some parent/child relationships are difficult in the extreme. They are bound up in all kinds of negative emotional, cultural, and biological energies. There just isn't enough love within the relationship to meet the larger body of fear, hatred, disappointment, shame, and guilt. Looking at this situation with sentimentality only leads to further distress. You can't really live on the hope that things will get better when the underlying conditions deny it. It's okay to drop your pursuit of any accommodation at all. Sometimes we need to acknowledge a hopeless situation for what it is, and then let go of it and go on from there.

By totally letting go, you will gain a tremendous amount of psychic energy. Letting go creates a new beginning out of which you can radiate loving kindness and help to heal things from a psychological distance. You are *not* obliged to create fairy-tale endings in your life, or to run into your mother's arms with both of you streaming tears of pent-up joy. Even when that happens in the movies, they don't show us how things turn out after that peak moment!

You are obliged, however, to do the wisest thing you can. Sometimes the karma of a relationship requires stepping far, far back from it. In doing so, you may also free your mother. But be very careful that you don't step away with the intention to make things better for her. Step out of the relationship in order to create an opening for a new beginning.

Q: I am nineteen and am living at home with my parents and attending the university. I feel that I've lived at home too long, but financial circumstances demand that I stay there for one more year. Then I should be free to live somewhere close to the campus.

The tension level in my parents' house is so high that I just want to scream. I need more room, more freedom. What can I do to survive the next twelve months?

A: If you are feeling so stressed at home, your parents are probably feeling the same and are on the verge of blowing their lids as well. If you can live in a more skillful way, the situation will cool down. How to do this? By radiating love to everyone in the house.

Life is like this at nineteen years of age. It is a difficult time. You have arrived at the age of responsibility. This is just the beginning of meeting difficult situations as a responsible adult. There will be challenges along the way, regardless of what kind of lifestyle you choose and what kind of economic and social status surrounds your life. If there were no difficulties, you would be flowing along free of karmic influences, and in fact wouldn't have been born into this realm at all.

This being so, you must learn how to gather your mental and physical resources to deal with difficulties, patiently enduring them, intelligently and sensitively making the most of them, and honoring them for the opportunities they provide for you. None of the demands that difficulties present asks that you judge yourself on the results. You simply do the best you can. If the best you can isn't sufficient for the situation, life will throw it back for you to meet again.

So, understand your situation from a greater perspective. Don't think that what is happening to you is unfair or unjustified; what is happening to you at all times is just what should be happening. Your situation at home is an opportunity for learning. See it that way. Begin to make the best out of the opportunity by being more careful. Watch your mind. Don't let a small irritation go unnoticed, for it is the small irritations that build into deep resentment. When there is enough anger in the air, war is inevitable. Be a peacemaker. To be a peacemaker you need only to be someone who doesn't generate violent mental states.

One last comment for you to reflect upon: When the kettle is about to boil, remember that sometimes we just have to clench our teeth, retreat from a heated situation, and go out for a brisk walk around the block. This too can be a manifestation of love in action.

Q: Has your relationship with your parents grown warmer and closer, now that you live the gentle life of a monastic?

A: Though I am living a good life as a monk, this hasn't changed the perception my parents have of me. I grew up in one of those toxic families that is full of confusion and abuse. Twenty years ago I decided that I would only visit my parents if I could stay in a motel or a separate apartment. The situation has not changed. Regardless of how much I have developed and matured as a person, my parents have chosen to remain in a time-warp and still regard me as an obstinate adolescent unwilling to live my life according to their ideas and expectations. Such is karma.

Through meditation I have become content with this situation and don't expect it to be any more than it is. I no longer feel disappointed or feel it is my job to make everything okay. This is what I mean when I say things are as they are. Wisdom is simply being in alignment with things as they are. Nothing more, nothing special.

The ability to assume a stance of nonattachment in one's family relationships comes from reflecting on and penetrating through the deceptive nature of conventional ideas. By doing this exercise often and consistently, one discovers that roles such as mother, father, husband, wife, sister, and brother are deeply embedded social and cultural constructs. Eventually we see that these are labels we ourselves superimpose. In essence, there isn't really any self who those labels apply to.

Wisdom allows us to step back from clinging relationships and their vagaries. This does not mean that one should refuse to recognize one's family duties or to express appreciation for the goodness of one's family. Rather, it offers one the restful spaciousness to allow all family members to grow in their own unique ways.

If our parents don't love us, it is because they don't see us, or they see us incorrectly. They need only to love us for who we are, not for what we do or what we believe in. Find your own way, no matter how much it isolates you. You can never be happy by living only to make others happy.

Q: So many of the questions people ask you are about relationships. Why is this?

A: Modern people suffer a great deal over relationships. This is a major source of anxiety in present-day Western culture, and as globalization seeps into Asia, it is becoming more of a problem here too. In the not-too-distant past, say ten to fifteen years ago, this wasn't a problem here at all.

People keep wanting something for themselves out of a relationship. It won't work that way. The selfishness of wanting something for yourself creates the need to do something to make it happen. The tangle only gets tighter. This is the common, mistaken idea that we can make something work by doing, rather than by letting go. As long as two people are each pulling the world toward themselves, there will be an endless struggle to find peace and happiness in that relationship.

The secret to making a relationship work is to reduce the number of needy persons in the relationship by one.

The root of the problem is that people no longer know how to relate to themselves. They don't know who they are, where they are going, what the point of this existence is, whether they should marry and have children or stay single and enjoy their freedom, and so on. With their own lives uncertain, they can hardly be expected to be able to build and sustain a healthy relationship with another. Even close friendships cannot be established in this milieu of confusion and anxiety. People often remain emotionally close to their nuclear family and have a ring of acquaintances who they see occasionally.

Meditation is a path that provides access to understanding and wisdom. Meditation allows us to slow things down enough to penetrate the confusion and to see things that have been hidden. We come to see the order and harmony in which things unfold. When we see how we ourselves fit into the world, we also recognize what makes relationships between people blend and flow. In the end, we come to understand that our responsibility is to learn to live in proper relationship with everything—that is, to relate with compassion and respect to everything in every moment.

Only wisdom can give us this understanding. Wisdom sees to it that our behavior is kind, loving, and appropriate. It is the force behind all spontaneous, appropriate actions.

CHAPTER THREE

Sexuality and Celibacy

Q: Is there a meditative approach to sexuality?

A: Of course. Observe where pleasant feelings come from. How do you respond to them? What is the result of the way you respond? Do you grasp and try to hold on to particular feelings and sensations? And what are the results of that grasping? What part does anticipation play in sexuality? What part does disappointment play?

As with any activity, the job of the meditator with regard to sex is to observe the mind. A vigilant meditator will always find something interesting and profound to notice.

Q: When I was younger I used to enjoy the sexual feelings and images that would spontaneously pass through my mind and body. Now I find them disturbing. Previously, they came up when I talked to or thought about a person who was attractive to me. That seems fair enough. But now they come up when I have business with people whom I really don't find so attractive and who are much older than I am. That this is happening as I get older is alarming to me. What is this all about?

A: Who can say? Karma. An abandonment of discrimination prompted by the media, which exalts sexuality. Or lust, or hormones, or a combination of the above. Or even premature menopause, which is a reality in males as well as in females.

Some people fall into a compulsion around alcohol, others around music. Others around sports, or travel. The effect in all cases is a feeling of being swallowed up by energies that are hard to control yet capture our attention and enslave our behavior.

If the mind is captivated by sexuality and continually seasoned by media images, it is naturally going to kick on its romantic movie machinery every time it encounters an appealing form. We see what we consider to be a beautiful image, and the whole affair rolls out in the twinkling of a moment. A romantic dinner, a stroll in the park, holding hands, the first kiss—here is that somebody who can save me! I finally found Ms. or Mr. Right.

When dealing with challenges such as this one, you must be willing to let go quickly. Don't allow your mind to fantasize or your thoughts to proliferate. Notice how the process of letting go loosens the grip of these energies ever so slightly. This breaks the pattern. You must be determined and resolute in letting go. In my experience, this may mean that we sometimes have to just grit our teeth and refuse to go along with infatuation, adolescent curiosity, and the like.

Observe how some of the images associated with pleasure come back quickly and quietly. Let go again and again. Determination will gradually alter this situation dramatically. And we remain determined to change not so much because we no longer enjoy these feelings and images, but because we are fed up with being hooked by them.

Q: I find the idea of celibacy unnatural. I think celibates are people who are afraid of sex, have never experienced it, or think it is wrong. Celibacy seems to have only negative implications. What do you think?

A: The matter of celibacy is really quite troubling for most Westerners, perhaps because they feel threatened by it. It is not as if sexual experience is an unknown quality in the lives of celibates. Ninety percent of the celibate people I know have at least had affairs, even if they were never married. We all have experienced pleasure in these relationships. But whether we have come to recognize it or not, the disharmony and confusion that resulted from these relationships far outweighed the temporary delight.

Sexual activity is no insignificant life experience and is not something to be taken casually. Few Westerners actually understand the implications of sexual conduct. A teacher who would dare to advocate a long period of preparation and extended periods of abstinence would be ridiculed as old-fashioned and puritanical in today's society. Sexual relationships evoke all kinds of karmic energies. They involve our own karma, the karma of our partner, our previous partner's karma, our partner's previous partner's karma, and so on. That means that all former exploitative, abusive, or inappropriate sexual behavior is involved in any present relationship. For everything happens in the present. This is no insignificant matter. It is no wonder that, more often than not, the results of impetuous sexuality are confusion and fragmentation. The ghosts of the past resurrect to overwhelm and confound us once again. This is why celibates welcome the opportunity to back off from sexuality.

Of course a sexual relationship that is grounded in bonding is wise sexuality, which comes about when there is maturity and commitment to live together and serve one another. Marriage creates a forum for this. Knowing this, most people choose to go through a marriage ceremony or other rite of acknowledgment so that their relationship is rooted to the earth.

In marriage, in celibacy, in friendship, in acquaintanceship, and all other human relationships, discipline around sexuality is critical. For celibates, that discipline takes the form of abstinence.

Suppose we have it wrong; suppose we have it backwards. Contrary to conventional wisdom, perhaps the standard ought to be: the less we have, the better off we are. The "less is more" principle can turn the world around. It could be that this business of seeking gratification through others' bodies is a trick. I bet you've suspected this at least once in your sexual experience.

If one gives it up, what is lost? Restlessness. Exploitation and the negative karma it produces. Dependency on others. And in some cases, the fear of loss, anxiety, and disappointment that come along with sexual relations. What could be gained? Time, energy, coolness, reflection upon oneself.

There is nothing to indicate, at least for me, that sexual activity is necessary for life. It is natural, yes. But so is abstinence. "Natural" isn't a very good criterion when it comes to choosing the way to freedom.

CHAPTER FOUR

Spiritual Education

Q: How can we, as parents, protect our children from the kinds of problems present in modern society?

A: I appreciate your concern. The world is more dangerous now than ever before. We are faced not only with physical dangers but with emotional and psychological ones as well.

In reality, parents can protect their children from only a limited range of problems. Each child has his or her particular karma and experiences life accordingly. Children are vulnerable to influences from their environment and the people around them according to their karma. Thus, among a group of children whose parents are equally interested and involved in their children's activities, there will still always be some who will get involved in things like smoking and using drugs, while others will not be drawn into such foolish activities. Why is that? Simply said, it's because of karma.

So what can parents do to protect their children? They can show them the value of being good, kind, sensitive people by living virtuous lives themselves. Children learn best from the examples of people in their family circle. I recommend that parents teach their children the value of unselfishness, of patience, of contentment with what they have, and of diligence in their studies. A foundation of ethics paves the way for them to practice loving kindness in their adult lives. Meditation can also be gradually introduced into a child's routine as a natural way of bringing silence and balance into his or her life.

Our high-tech life demands that young people learn a range of skills—mastery of computers, business-oriented language, micro- and macro-economics, and so on—to prepare them for the job market. Political and environmental concerns contribute in a less formal way to the day-to-day menu of leading-edge information we are challenged to absorb. Almost every available erg of brain energy is required to keep up with all this and to compete with the more aggressive, ambitious kids sitting behind supercomputers, urged on by their fast-lane fathers. All this, plus the pervading presence of television, produces an overloaded, saturated, complex mental world for young people to grow up in. It is a situation worthy of compassion.

This array of skills and expertise is of no benefit without ethical training. A young person's education must include an understanding of the role of virtue in human life, and a sense of fear and shame in doing what is universally considered unskillful and inappropriate. Otherwise, the inner system that holds human beings to the track of kindness and goodness will be overridden. The lives of these young people will zoom out of control into the dangerous areas of human relationship, for they are then not so much living a life as skidding along on two wheels unmonitored by conscience, creating heavy karma as they fumble along with their immature desires.

An education integrated with ethics promotes the maturing of young people into decent, sensitive adults who are able and willing to take responsibility for the situations they encounter in their personal lives. They will grow up to be people able to uplift the world rather than add more dead weight to it. The planet is already swollen with problems, and there are few honest, ethical leaders able to take the ball and patiently move us toward the goal. The need of the age is to improve the lives of the world's family and rectify the problems that threaten the planet. Only compassionate wisdom can do the job.

My own list of qualities that are important to a child's development includes: skill in choosing virtuous friends, nonexploitation of others, loyal companionship, responsibility, generosity, inclination toward doing good, shedding bad habits, interest in purifying the mind, endurance, patience, contentment, the courage to keep out of trouble, and acceptance of criticism. If these are introduced into children's education, we could be confident that we are moving into the next century with a population of competent young people who have balanced modern technological skills with moral integrity. These two have to go hand in hand if the planet is to continue as a livable environment.

Q: My son is a bright, curious little boy. He seems to be exceptionally intelligent and bent on discovering the nature of the world. I've been thinking he should have the opportunity to begin meditation as soon as possible. Is there a best time for a child to begin practicing meditation?

A: Children are the magical people of the human race. Give your son room to explore the world, the more space the better. I don't know of anyone who can say at what age a child should begin meditation. However, if he starts too early, he may learn an important posture but won't understand the point of it, nor the possibilities. He will get the peel, but not the fruit.

You need to wait, really, until the trouble-making machinery is set up and suffering begins in earnest. Until then, support his curiosity through appreciation of his interest in the sensory world. Try to inculcate in him the sense that the world is ultimately an enigma, even though some adults may pretend to understand it.

If he understands early that conventional wisdom is a web of socially acceptable intellectual devices that form the structure of a culture, he will be able to maintain his vibrant curiosity in the face of factors that try to make the world black and white. In this way his mind will be established in the right attitude for meditation. Be his ally and the guardian of his spiritual aspirations. Help him to understand that he is inherently a conscious, spiritual, loving being, and that he has before him the unique opportunity to be free from suffering. When he understands this, he will himself direct his life toward ultimate freedom.

CHAPTER FIVE

Karma and Rebirth

Q: What is karma?

A: All religions recognize some kind of underlying principle that brings harmony to what appears to be chaos. In Buddhism, this primal energy that keeps the beat, providing a consistent rhythm to the manifestation of all form, is called karma.

Karma functions precisely as it does regardless of how or from where the world came into being, if it came into being at all. Rather than trying to answer questions about the origins of the universe, the theory of karma is a recognition of the principle running the system.

Living ethically helps us to make the best out of the karmic situation that so completely determines the conditions of our life. Do good, and goodness shall follow. Do what is not so good, and reap the results of that as well.

Q: Why is life so unfair? The selfish, arrogant, and power-ful seem to live as they want to, enjoying whatever they want without concern for others, whereas sensitive, kind people seem to experience more than their fair share of difficulty and pain. Thus it seems more sensible to try to get whatever you can out of this life.

A: The world is painfully and precisely fair. The world you are experiencing is as it is because the karma you made for your-self was as it was. We have free choice, you know. But once nega-tive karma has been generated from our choices, it is ours to keep. No one else, nothing else, can interfere to change the effect it bears on our lives.

The seemingness of other people's lives is just that. Some-times someone else's life seems to be a winner. But we see in effect only one or two frames of a very long movie. Seen from a broader and deeper perspective, the picture may be completely different. Many of the so-called winners these days appear to me like lead-ing characters in a "B" comedy movie.

We are the result of our karma. Karma is a neutral, emo-tionless mechanism that merely collects the results of inten-tional actions and returns them to their respective owners. This may not happen within the frames of the movie you are ob-serving, but sooner or later the appropriate karmic conse-quences will manifest. Simply stated, this is the law of the universe. Everyone, without exception, gets their just desserts—

and they may not necessarily be sweet!

Q: Why do some people live well and long, and others briefly and tragically?

A: People live their lives according to the tendencies determined by their karma. They live as long as they do and as well as they do according to their *punya,* the merit they accrue from good deeds.

This is completely fair and just. If someone with a storehouse of goodness behind them goes and squanders it, they will reap the consequences of that foolishness in direct relationship to their carelessness. Don't worry if others don't seem to be getting their just desserts. They will. And so will you. Now is the time to do good, live wisely, support wisdom, have loving compassion for others, and develop your mind as best you can.

Q: In Asia many people believe that their condition is caused by karma. That means that poor people working for just enough to survive are destined to live in a world of poverty their entire lives. They are bound by the idea that because they are poor, they must die poor as well. This notion itself must contribute heavily to the cycle of poverty in many Asian countries.

A: Few people really understand the mechanism of karma.

One has to know where to look. I must say that your way of view-
ing karma in Asia is rather over-simplified. Westerners' notions of
karma often reveal an attitude of cultural superiority that perceives the principle of karma as part of a religion based on fatal-
ism and superstition.

Karma is a natural law. It operates in nature whether anyone recognizes it or not. The law of karma reveals the complexity
of the problems of chronic poverty in the lives of very poor people.
In the West, many have the idea that money and market-based
job training will bring an end to poverty, that people will then be
in a position to earn an adequate living and eventually move up
the social ladder. However, if we recognize that poverty is the result of negative karma, we see that the vast majority of poor people
have a whole spectrum of obstacles in front of them. It's not that
they have been indoctrinated into the assumption of a predes-
tined fate and that's the whole of it; in fact, they have heavy karma
to bear throughout this life.

People born into a cycle of poverty struggle through the
minimum level of schooling until they can quit to find a job. In a
country like Thailand, a boy or girl can continue in school through
the aid of scholarships. However, poor children usually leave
school before they become literate. They retain a diminished self-
concept of their intellectual abilities. They usually lack ambition
and enthusiasm for education or work. They are born into family
situations that condition them to see only a tiny range of work
possibilities. They think about work in terms of days and seasons,
so they don't try to improve careless and sloppy habits. When
they acquire more money than they need, they promptly spend
it. They are also easily addicted to alcohol, tobacco, and gam-
bling. Poverty is a condition in which whole constellations of

heavy, negative forces keep people in a circumscribed, survival-oriented existence.

We recognize this as the ill-effects of unwholesome karma. It is, of course, possible to work one's way out, but it is a long, hard, uphill struggle. As spiritual advisors, we try hard to teach people how to live skillfully and morally in order to avoid such a tragic kind of existence.

Q: I don't know whether I should believe in rebirth or believe that we are only born once. Rebirth is much more fashionable among my circle of friends, but I don't have a clue regarding either concept.

A: We can believe in either, both, or neither. A variety of views and opinions about this have developed over the centuries. They all have their adherents. Some believe so fervently that things are as they believe them to be that they would kill to defend their beliefs. This is so irrational that we can only shake our heads in wonder.

All these views and opinions lie within the same straitjacket called belief. Keep in mind that they are merely *ideas* about the world and are subject to change; they have no real substance. If you want to know about rebirth, or even about no-birth, you will need to turn your mind toward the source of these concepts and learn to see through or even beyond rational perception.

Walking with my eyes cast down just in front of me, I move through the villages while the day is still in its infancy. As I pass along the streets, people call out an invitation to accept their food offerings. Sometimes I come upon a pair of feet that jars my memory back to some obscure time or place. Gazing at what I take to be an old man's funny assortment of toes takes me back to some other lifetime, some other plane of existence. Yet the notion of past lives is impossible to endorse with any degree of confidence, for who among us can really know this directly? Some other life or life form may suggest itself, but that doesn't make it real. These quirky memory blips could simply be a trick of the imagination. People can get caught up in these nebulous concepts. In reality, everything that vaguely suggests itself is merely a possibility in a world of infinite possibilities. None of this has any bearing on our predicament right here and right now.

The rational mind lowers itself from its exalted position whenever we consider the immensity of the physical universe. Pulling ourselves away from our computers and TVs to look up at the stars twinkling on a clear night, we can't help but be humbled by the awesome nature of the world we live in. This is a vastly different mode of mind than the one that worries about the endless array of petty concerns pertaining to this one life. It makes us wonder, "Did I come from somewhere up there? Out there?" We all seem to have a sense that this life is not all that we have experienced or will experience.

All this leads to thoughts about rebirth and all its fascinating implications. Was I once the Queen of Sheba? Napoleon? Sam the tailor? There are endless possibilities and we can embrace them all and, in a flight of fantasy, extricate ourselves from being whoever it is we now think we are.

Just for a moment consider these two hypotheses: One is that we are born once through the merging of an egg and sperm. The life that arises out of that meeting lasts at most a hundred years, and then it disappears. The other hypothesis takes shape through sustained meditation practice. Consciousness is capable and indeed susceptible to taking birth in any kind of form, both imaginable and unimaginable. In reality, everything exists at all times. We have existed in an endless series of forms by way of an energy dimension that has nothing whatsoever to do with our notion of time and space. Since everything exists at all times, it may be possible to be simultaneously alive in a body and not so. All things are one thing and all time is now.

CHAPTER SIX

Looking Death Squarely in the Eye

Q: Two years ago, a neighbor's infant daughter died quite suddenly in the middle of the night. They had been yearning for this child for years and consequently were distraught to the point of madness when she died. Even now, two years later, they still mourn her and just can't seem to get back to their lives. What can be done for them?

A: As trite as it may sound, I can only say to let time do the healing. If the parents are not meditators, it is unlikely that they can convert this traumatic occasion into awareness of the nature of life. We just have to leave the task of healing to the one that does it best—time.

However, since you have been meditating for some years, I can speak more directly to you, knowing that you will not regard what I say as callous. I believe that we all have experienced this kind of heart-wrenching pain again and again over the course of

173

many, many lifetimes. I can empathize. But I also now know where the suffering comes from. You see, the devastation that the parents feel comes from loving their baby too much. Anything taken to the extreme, even love, generates a proportionately exaggerated response, such as an overwhelming fear of loss. In this particular situation, the parents' affection went over the top and the pain of loss was magnified beyond endurance, as it would be with anything or anyone we love too much.

Q: A distant relative of mine died last month, and I was obliged to attend the funeral. It was a really strange experience. This man, who was very wealthy, was despised by most of the people who came to the funeral because of his stinginess. I suppose that, like me, most of them came out of curiosity. So I was quite surprised to see a lot of them crying. Isn't it odd how people respond in the presence of a corpse?

A: Yes, it is rather peculiar, and sad, that most people fall apart when confronted with death. At the root of their distress, of course, is fear—fear of their own inevitable destiny with death. A family that has cultivated spiritual awareness will meet death with dignity and equanimity. Certainly there will be sadness, but it will be an appropriate emotion that comes naturally from the pain of separation. When there is wisdom and mature love, there will be space between sorrow and hysteria. This tempers the sadness so that the opportunity for reflection is not lost and a funeral can become an occasion for reflecting on the inevitable ending of our life. These events can serve as prompts to remind us to live every moment skillfully in the little bit of time remaining to us.

Q: As far back as I can remember, I have been haunted by the fear of death. Even as a little girl in kindergarten, the thought of death always troubled me. I would be afraid that the building I was in might collapse under me or that someone might come into my bedroom at night and kill me. These images have turned me into a fear-ridden person. Is it possible to meditate my way out of this insecure feeling?

A: I would begin by saying that mature meditation practice will take you beyond the fear of death, both neurotic and actual, for we come to see that the death we commonly consider the end of physical life is just that. The body loses its ability to preserve itself in this environment, but consciousness, which is immaterial and not struggling to maintain itself, remains as it is. Ultimately, then, death of the body is just the natural and inevitable outcome of birth. It couldn't be otherwise. And if you think about it, who wants an aged and disintegrating body that has become so old that none of the senses work any longer?

Much of our fear of death is cultural. We learn to be afraid of it. On the other hand, we also have a strong survival instinct that works continuously to keep us alive. We are wired by nature to survive as long as we need to. Governed by this primal instinct to survive, we continue to live as long as there is still enough life force in the body to deal with illness and trauma.

Fear of death is an add-on. It comes about only because ignorance overrides awareness. Ignorance of this sort is the gross kind that is able to obscure the fact that we were born and that death is inevitable. Death must come sooner or later, in one way or another. In most cultures there is little in the way of education to remind us that the quality of life is the key to the success of our life, not its length. We are educated to fear death. Our societies have done a thorough job of convincing us that death is the great enemy. Perhaps you understood this as a child. Your fantasies of impending death were an outgrowth of the conflict between the reality of death and society's attempt to hide as a dark secret the fact that everyone must die, even infants who have just come into life.

I believe that it is very important for all of us to contemplate fear. What is the result of fear? Doesn't it make us cowardly and timid? Doesn't it provoke us into seeking a safe and secure life? Isn't that safe, secure life we strive for stagnant and boring? And isn't it true that stagnant and boring lives lead to indulgence, extravagance, and substance abuse? Isn't it true that the most static and staid lifestyles lead to severe depression? Finally, isn't it true that the appearance of any fear, even a trickle of fear, means that our minds are riddled with it, contaminating everything we do? These are questions we need to ponder so that we can understand our duties in life more accurately.

Through consistent meditation practice you educate the mind to understand the-way-things-are. As the mind moves from ignorance to truth, the individual quirks that harass us gradually fade away.

Q: I meditate regularly. Six months ago my mother died, and now my father has died suddenly. I was very close to both of them. When I sit in meditation, my eyes well up with tears and I feel overwhelmed with emotion. What can I do to get through this phase?

A: Keep practicing. This too will pass. What you are feeling is natural. If you keep practicing with wisdom, you will learn a lot about birth and death, attachment, and karma. What you are experiencing is the-way-things-are. Your parents still have a lot to offer you. Be wise and stay with the invitation.

Q: Do people die because of their karma?

A: People leave their bodies because of karma and, often, because of their carelessness, which is also connected with karma.

When any underlying factor necessary to support life is withdrawn or ceases, the body must die. When the supporting factors sustaining a life are strong, people are able to live long, healthy lives. However, most people live carelessly and negligently in both body and mind. They do not live in accord with nature. They don't develop their lives intelligently, and they don't take care of themselves in a manner that protects them from accidents and illness.

Everything—death as well as life—happens by the unseen causality of karma. Death is the end of a karmic phase. There is no need to see death as a calamity; so also there is little wisdom in rejoicing at the birth of a child.

Q: If the fear of death is so ingrained in our cultures, who benefits? Why is this as it is?

A: Perhaps it's because the fear of death is a basic tenet of materialism. Or because materialism thrives in an environment where death is the result of not having enough. Materialism is now the driving force of this world, so the fear of death is politically relevant. But we can leave the exploration of this to social scientists.

In the spiritual context, we consider this in a comprehensive way. We look beyond the conventional world. As meditators, we rely solely on experience in order to intuit reality. Our perspective isn't directed outside; it doesn't rely on books or authorities. Rather, we position ourselves to look within—to the mind. Then we can see how fear controls and even paralyzes us.

As we face fear, we see that it has no basis in ultimate reality, and therefore no basis in fact. Our fears arise out of a whole string of misguided perceptions, none of which makes any sense to an intelligent person. Under the influence of materialism coupled with desire we always want to possess something and take pride in it. We want to own everything we can forever as a symbol of our importance and success. By extension, we even want our bodies to be a source of envy. We want them to be eternally young, vigorous, beautiful, and vibrant. Hence, the vitamin, supplemental food, and health spa industries.

From the viewpoint of a biologist or a physicist, this is all absurd. Scientifically, the body exists momentarily as a collection of elements. It is held together by electrical cohesion. In reality, the body comes apart and re-forms every moment. The body we are using is an aggregate of various bits of energy. What we think to be our body is in fact earth, air, fire, and water. The molecules forming this body die and are reborn billions of times in a day. Death is continuous! Wisdom looks at the fear of death as a joke. It is no more to be feared than life. The two are inseparably paired.

What vanquishes fear is clear understanding. In Buddhism we call the most profoud kind of understanding "realization"— the ability to recognize the real. Fear is based on ignorance, the opposite of realization. Of course, there are things to be concerned about in the world and to take intelligent precautions to protect ourselves from, but when the mind is balanced, awake, and alert, this will happen naturally.

However, when the mind is bombarded with TV images of violence and video images of mayhem, the mind loses perspective and falls into confusion. It's not surprising, is it? This mind can no longer discriminate between natural reality and fantasy. If things reach that point, we cannot discern the feelings that arise naturally regarding our mortality. Movie scenes and war photos become mixed up with various existential feelings regarding the dilemma of being embodied in this world. Memory, instinct, and a natural awareness of the-way-things-are become entangled, and we no longer know what is real and what is conditioned. The result of this confusion is doubt, which is associated with fear. For if doubt clouds the mind, there isn't enough inner light to really know what is what. There is no vibrant confidence to rely upon. Fear makes its way into all spheres of the rational mind, and so we live with fear continuously. It is so close and so pervasive that we no longer even notice it.

If our life is made up of fear on one side and desire on the other—for they come and go together—we are living in virtual slavery. With meditation we try to free ourselves from both.

Q: There is a lot of interest in death and dying these days, demonstrated in the many books on the subject. I haven't had a chance to read any of them. However, now it looks like I may have the opportunity to facilitate this passage for a relative and for a close friend. How can I use my meditation experience to help them?

A: Yes, books on this subject abound. From what I hear, many are skillfully written and approach death intelligently. You can read them to get an overview.

If you are working with people who are not Buddhists or who don't think quite the same way you do, you have to be particularly sensitive and careful. You are only going to be helpful in this situation if you approach it as an opportunity to help others. You won't be helpful if you have a hidden agenda.

Right from the beginning you will need to understand that you will only truly serve if you stay alert and sensitive to the timely needs of your friends. You want to try and come into their lives when they are ready to be open to whatever you have to offer. Your job is to prepare everything by being kind, comforting, and compassionate. To do this you can really only rely on the depth of your meditation practice.

Q: The friend who I am speaking about has recently become a Buddhist. We have been close friends for a long time.

A: It would benefit him greatly if he could come to recognize death for what it really is. You could present death as a natural conclusion to a beginning, which in turn initiates another new beginning. This helps to reduce the anxiety and fear around death. The great challenge for someone in your position is to communicate that in the ultimate spiritual sense no one really dies. But how deeply do you know this? You won't be able to communicate it more deeply than you yourself realize it. So this may be your work in this process. Come to understand the fact of death in your own heart. Anyone who wants to help others should prepare themselves first. Your understanding of truth communicates itself.

Q: Is death the end of all this?

A: Death as we think of it culturally is a concept that you had to learn to believe in. Because it is a belief, you can learn to disbelieve it as well. The notion of death as the end of life is fueled by your belief system. Investigate this. Find out who it is that believes such things and then builds their life around it. Contemplate this and you will learn a lot about the-way-things-are.

If you are asking if the body stops functioning, if it quits responding to the environment as it normally does, the answer is a definite yes. That's obvious. On the other hand, the idea that death is the end of all this, though it is deeply ingrained in many of us, is just an *idea* that your contemplation can penetrate beyond.

This question is a profound one that you will carry with you all your life. Examining it can shatter all kinds of misperceptions you carry regarding the world. You will see that death and life are partners, twins. Death cannot be the end of life, just as life isn't the end of death. Right now, how much death is occurring in your body? Someday you will come to understand the truth about death and that truth will set you free.

A good Buddhist eulogy could read like this: "This is as far as I got." There is ultimately only one thing to accomplish, and it is an on-going, life-to-life process.

One's consciousness at death is the only measure of a life's accomplishment. If someone in critical condition with a mind still functioning is able to hear this and contemplate upon it, it could be an invaluable gift. Much depends on how well a person has prepared for the last moments in this body. Obviously, if someone has led a careless and negligent life for decades, there won't be the lucidity and alert circumspection to look clearly into the nature of death. Instead, there will be a proliferation of worries around lengthening survival. Hospitals reinforce this anxiety. Their dread of death creates a maze of machinery and intervention. This is the karma of a life lodged in the mainstream modern world, with all the requisite insurance policies.

Still, if someone regards the moment of death as momentous and is prepared to realize that all that has happened in the span of their life is but a prelude to the dying moment, their dedication to inner investigation and one-pointed concentration could initiate a flash of insight that has a profound effect. We could say, then, that these final hours in our human life places us on the brink of Buddhahood.

QUEST BOOKS
are published by
The Theosophical Society in America
Wheaton, Illinois 60189-0270
a branch of a world organization
dedicated to the promotion of the unity of
humanity and the encouragement of the study of
religion, philosophy, and science, to the end that
we may better understand ourselves and our place in
the universe. The Society stands for complete
freedom of individual search and belief.
For further information about its activities,
write, call 1-800-669-1571, or consult its Web page:
http://www.theosophical.org

*The Theosophical Publishing House
is aided by the generous support of
THE KERN FOUNDATION,
a trust established by Herbert A. Kern
and dedicated to Theosophical education.*